YORK

Exprimit Ecclesiæ fidei candore nitentes.
THO. GENT

EX LIBRIS

'You nearly
had him that time...'
and other cricket stories

'You nearly had him that time...'
and other cricket stories

Fred Trueman
and Frank Hardy

Illustrated by David Langdon

Stanley Paul
London Melbourne Sydney Auckland Johannesburg

The wicket was intact...

Stanley Paul & Co. Ltd

An imprint of the Hutchinson Publishing Group

3 Fitzroy Square, London W1P 6JD

Hutchinson Group (Australia) Pty Ltd
30–32 Cremorne Street, Richmond South, Victoria 3121
PO Box 151, Broadway, New South Wales 2007

Hutchinson Group (NZ) Ltd
32–34 View Road, PO Box 40–086, Glenfield, Auckland 10

Hutchinson Group (SA) (Pty) Ltd
PO Box 337, Bergvlei 2012, South Africa

First published 1978
Second impression December 1978
Third impression February 1980
©Frank Hardy and Frederick Trueman 1978

Illustrations © David Langdon 1978

Printed in Great Britain by The Anchor Press Ltd
and bound by Wm Brendon & Son Ltd
both of Tiptree, Essex

ISBN 0 09 133680 5

Contents

Preface:
About Fred Trueman and
Cricket Yarns

Frank Hardy

In one of his famous after-dinner speeches about cricket, Fred Trueman said: 'Cricket has more funny stories than any other game. And, as they pass down through history, they become exaggerated.'

Well, he ought to know! The majority of the stories in this book come from Fred – and they are extremely funny and skilfully exaggerated. They say much about the rarified world of the professional cricketer and the folklore of the people who play and watch the grand old game. And they display the yarn-spinner's eye for the absurdity of man's most serious endeavours, the irreverent aside and the revealing punchline.

I met Fred Trueman for the first time when we began work on this book. Our meeting was suggested by an old friend of Fred's, the former Australian all-rounder, Keith Miller.

Having in mind to attempt a book of humorous cricket stories, I had approached Keith Miller in the Steyne Hotel, in Manly, near Sydney and asked him to collaborate.

Keith replied: 'Well, I would like to – but there is only one man for that job, Freddie Trueman. He knows more yarns about cricket than you could poke a stick at. You fancy yourself as a yarn-spinner; well, wait until you've heard Fred.'

.Having the dubious honour of being Australia's champion yarn-spinner (I wrested the title from Tall Tale Tex Tyrell in an epic twelve-hour battle in the Hotel Darwin), I was fairly confident that I could hold my own even with the lad from the Yorkshire dales himself.

When Fred and I eventually met in London, I was very much aware of being with a man who had become a legend in his own lifetime and who had been my cricket idol. That Fred Trueman was the greatest fast bowler of all time is, I think, beyond argument. He could bowl as fast as Harold Larwood and, with conditions to suit, swing the ball as much as Alan Davidson. And he was the first bowler in history to take 300 Test wickets.

But my admiration for him had been as much for the man of legend as for the cricketer.

When you meet a hero at first hand, you are apt to be let down. But Fred Trueman didn't disappoint me: it was all there, the earthy wit, the outrageous sense of humour, the devil-may-care attitude of the man who doffs his cap to no one and, of course, the story teller's idiom.

We soon had a glass of beer in hand and warmed to each other and the task of compiling this book.

Over a period of months, we spent much time together, including a week at his house in Yorkshire, with Veronica feeding us and laughing at our jokes.

At the beginning, I had suggested that we turn the funny side of cricket into short stories which could sum up the men and manners of the game. And we found that cricket, like grand opera, is often funniest when an exaggerated twist throws unexpected light on its deadly earnestness.

As the book emerged from the fumes of our pipes, the froth of the beer and the whirring of the tape recorder, the stories were many and varied.

First and foremost, Fred's own account of funny incidents in his career, like the outrageous tale of that Test Match in the West Indies; and second, the yarns he has picked up, made up or polished up over the years, like the one about Mick Cowan's encounter with Wes Hall.

The third kind are the stories about Fred Trueman, like the one in which he receives a telegram from his Air Force Commanding Officer during his third Test Match (probably true); and the one about his encounter with the World's Worst Cricket Umpire at Wagga Wagga in Australia (almost certainly not true).

The fourth type of story, I enjoyed the most: the ones in which we created an immortal cricketing type. 'The Flucker' is in this category.

Next, are the stories made up from bits and pieces of

incidents which have occurred or have been alleged to occur by imaginative yarn spinners, and making them into a story. Of these, 'The World's Best Cricket Umpire' is my favourite. And we are indebted to Peter Parfitt's reminiscences of the umpires he encountered for much of the fruity humour of this cautionary tale.

And last but not least, are the stories that have 'passed down through history' like the one about the cunning batsman who knocks a bail off when hooking.

Fred Trueman had one version of the yarn about the windy cricketer, I had another – then I met an old bloke in a pub at Wigan who had yet another which he swore he had actually witnessed. Has that incident happened in many places or have several yarn-spinners heard it and made their own version?

In the same vein, is the story of Bill Tallon's one day of glory at the Brisbane Cricket Ground: 'Bloody Beauty.' The yarn came to us from Neil Hawke, former Australian all-rounder now living in Yorkshire. He heard it from Wally Grout. Who did Wally Grout hear it from? Bill Tallon? I mean, did it actually happen?

Which raises the question: are any of these stories true? Well, apart from Fred's stories about himself, they are true enough – even if exaggerated as Fred has passed them down through history.

I tried to check up on one of the stories, 'How Sam Loxton was trapped at square leg'. A version of it was to be shown on Australian television, so I sent the script to Sam. Would he confirm or deny it?

Sam replied by letter: 'I must admit it makes a very good story – I don't believe you will convince anyone I could bat so long, but good luck with it.'

So I was none the wiser.

Were you present, dear reader, when one of these incidents occurred; have you been telling some of these stories for years?

We are perhaps in the area of myth and legend, of folk-lore, where stories emerge that are larger than life, truer than truth, to sum up all that is great and funny and fascinating – and ultimately ridiculous about the game called Cricket.   St Paul-de-Vence December 1977

1

The Worst Batsman Who Ever Played

Fred Trueman

When I played for Yorkshire we had a character in the side called Michael Cowan. Mick was a good fast left-hand bowler, the worst batsman who ever played, and a very funny man.

In 1963, Mick was bowling at the other end to me when Yorkshire played the West Indies at Middlesbrough. We gave them a right going over and won by ten wickets.

After that match they said: 'Just wait till we get you Yorkshire so-and-sos at Sheffield. We're going to murder you.'

Well, fair enough. You can do nout about it when something like that is said by Charlie Griffiths and Wes Hall, can you? You have to be careful: they are each built like a brick chicken-house.

So we got to Sheffield and – sure enough – the West Indies have put their full Test side in against us. And they didn't half give us a lacing, didn't they, not half. They hammered us all over Bramall Lane.

Anyway, in the last innings of the match, we are eight wickets down and, with four minutes to go before stumps, Wes Hall began what could be the last over.

And we're trying to save the match, aren't we? It's about twenty-six past six. And I'm at the non-striker's end.

Wes Hall sent one down and it broke the off stump into about seven pieces.

We were nine wickets down – with only Mick Cowan to come. No way known he can play five balls from West Hall.

And Mick came out the gate carrying his bat. Now, the only reason Mick carried a bat was because he thought he had to. He knew little about the coarse art of batting and nothing about the finer points.

As Mick came to the wicket, I said to him: 'Mick, for God's sake, we've got to try to make this the last over, so we've got to take our time – and not get out. Tell you what, see if you can get a single off the first ball, then I'll try to play four balls from Wes Hall.'

Mick said nothing but he went to a lot of trouble, taking guard twice.

Then I walked down the wicket and started throwing bits of grass and stuff off the pitch, wasting time. That's not unsporting, it's known as gamesmanship.

Suddenly, Frankie Worrell, the West Indies Captain said: 'Fred, you're at the non-striker's end, aren't you?'

And I admitted: 'Yes.'

And Frankie said: 'Well, what are you cleaning the wicket for?'

I replied: 'To make sure my mate, Mick, doesn't get too nervous.'

The umpire said: 'Come on, Fred.'

And, at last, Mick Cowan said: 'I'm ready.'

Well, by this time, Wes Hall was out in Cherry Street to start his run up. He came down the pavilion steps onto the ground. And he was running at nearly 200 miles an hour down that slope at Bramall Lane.

And he let one go, did Wes, at Mick Cowan, who played down the leg stump. The ball went over the off stump.

Mick looked up the wicket at me and he said: 'I think this fella has found my weakness, Fred.'

And I said: 'Yeh.'

And he's back in Cherry Street, is Wes, and he came in again – and Mick played down the off stump. The ball went over the leg stump.

And I said: 'It looks to me he's found both of 'em now, Mick.'

But we were not going too badly. Only two balls and one minute to go; and there was no way that with his long run up Wes Hall can bowl them in time to give the West Indies another over. We might save the game yet, I thought. But, of course, all Wes had to do was get Mick out.

By this time, Frankie Worrell had got the message. He

placed all ten fielders right around Mick in a tight little circle, and there's just a gap between silly mid-on and silly mid-off for the ball to come through.

And Mick Cowan was standing in the middle of it, shaking like an aspen leaf.

And Wes Hall was about half way through his run up when Mick put his hand up and said: 'Stop!'

And the umpire said: 'What's the matter now, Mick?'

And Mick Cowan said: 'I'll tell you what the matter is: if this lot don't move back, I'm going to appeal against the light.'

Appeal against the light

2

'But he smells nice'

Fred Trueman

One of the legendary characters of English County Cricket was a man by the name of Emmott Robinson.

Emmott was a professional and a fast bowler. The only thing he liked about batsmen was getting them out – especially if they were amateurs and gentlemen.

Once, before the war, he was playing for Yorkshire against Cambridge at the Cambridge University ground.

Cambridge won the toss and batted.

The old Emmott opened the bowling for Yorkshire as he always did in the 1920s.

Soon, Cambridge were ten runs for three wickets, and Emmott had taken two of them.

And he was ready and keen for his next wicket, the old Emmott.

And who does he see walking down the steps of the pavilion? Only the future amateur Captain of England: A.E.R. Gilligan, his gentlemanly self.

Yes, he's there coming in next, is Gilligan.

And he's got on a brand-new Cambridge blue cap; a brand-new Viyella shirt; a brand-new pair of Simpson cream trousers; brand-new Cotton Oxford boots; a brand-new pair of Graham Nicholls pads; brand-new silk batting gloves.

And a brand-new bat; never before used.

As Gilligan strode, proud and superior, towards the wicket, someone asked Emmott Robinson: 'What's this fella doing, then?'

And Emmott replied: 'I don't know, but he smells nice.'

So he got to the crease, did Gilligan, and he looked around to see where the fielders were.

Eventually, he put down his bat and said: 'Mister umpire, could I have two legs?'

And the umpire said: 'Certainly, Mister Gilligan. A little away from you, a little more. That is two legs, Mister Gilligan.'

Touching his cap (as they did in those days), A.E.R. Gilligan said: 'Thank you, Mister umpire.'

So Gilligan made his mark, scratched it with the toe of his boot. Then he had another look around to make sure none of the crafty Yorkshire devils had moved while he was taking his guard.

Suddenly, a voice shouted: 'Come on, let's get on with bloody game.'

It was Emmott Robinson with both feet in the resin box.

But A.E.R. Gilligan again put his bat down and asked: 'Am I still on two legs, Mister umpire?'

'You are, Mister Gilligan,' the umpire answered.

And Gilligan said: 'Thank you very much indeed. I'm ready.'

The umpire said: 'Play.'

And in comes Emmott Robinson with the first ball, an absolute smasher: just as it pitched on the middle stump, it swung away sharply and cart-wheeled the off stump about four yards out of the ground.

Well, he couldn't believe it, couldn't A.E.R. Gilligan, the future amateur Captain of England. He looked down at the broken wicket in amazement.

But being an amateur and a gentleman, he tucked his bat under his arm and began to walk back to the pavilion, taking off his silk gloves as he went.

And, as he walked past Emmott Robinson, A.E.R. Gilligan, gracious and condescending, said: 'Well bowled indeed, Robinson. That was a great ball.'

And Emmott Robinson replied: 'Aye – but it were wasted on thee.'

3

Famous Last Words: 'I never played cricket on a windier day'

Fred Trueman

A certain cunning County cricketer – it might have been anybody – was always trying to trick umpires into not giving him out, wasn't he.

He had a trick for every occasion. If a fast ball hit his glove and was caught by the wicket keeper, he would rub his hip vigorously.

On a very windy day at Headingley, he played back to a fast one and touched the leg stump with his heel.

One of the bails trembled and just fell softly off.

As quick as a flash, the cunning batsman said to the umpire: 'Hell, that wind is strong! I never played cricket on a windier day.'

'Aye, you're right,' the umpire at the bowler's end said. 'It is very windy. In fact, you want to be careful it doesn't blow your cap off on your way back to the pavilion. I saw you walk on that wicket and I'm giving you out.'

4

'You nearly had him that time...'

Frank Hardy

On the cricket field, if there was one thing Freddie Trueman disliked more than batsmen, then that was umpires. Yes, he really disliked umpires, did Fred.

He once said: 'A strange breed of animals, umpires.'

He tried to intimidate them with loud appeals, glares, sarcastic remarks and muttered abuse. He claimed that he suffered from bad umpiring, of being stuffed out of sight by umpires, especially in Australia and the West Indies.

Of course, Freddie more than held his own with batsmen – and umpires. That is, until he came up against the World's Worst Cricket Umpire, One-eyed Mick McConkidale, in Wagga Wagga, New South Wales, during the 1958-9 English tour of Australia.

It was Freddie's first trip to Australia and he was very popular with the crowds. Usually Australian cricket supporters don't like Pom fast bowlers (Harold Larwood was about as popular as a temperance advocate at a publicans' picnic), but Freddie had that devil-may-care attitude which appeals to Australians, and he played the game hard but fairly.

He also displayed a great sense of humour: on Foundation Day at the Adelaide Oval, when the traditional twenty-gun salute began at the near-by military base, Freddie held his heart after the first shot, staggered after the second, fell to the ground after the third – and held up his handkerchief like a white flag after the fourth. And he won over even the spectators on the Hill at Sydney – and they would, as Freddie himself put it, make the Stretford End at Manchester look like a meeting of the Band of Hope. They baited Freddie and he threw a few wisecracks right back, informing them that their ancestors came from the best jails in Britain – amongst other things. Then one of the Hillites offered Freddie a can of Fosters which the lad gargled to the cheers of the crowd, didn't he?

So apart from a few bad decisions, Freddie had a great time and took twenty wickets, though he played in only three Tests.

Of course, the Pom selectors and Captain, amateurs and gentlemen all, treated Freddie Trueman as the team's work-horse, never stopped bowling him as if he were a bloody machine. So, at the end of the tour, he accepted an invitation to rest for a few days on the property of an English sheep farmer near Wagga Wagga. And that's where he met One-eyed Mick McConkidale.

One-eyed Mick was a cricket umpire in the Wagga Wagga district; for the Wagga Wagga team itself, in fact, because each team had its own umpire in those days. Mick gave a lot of bad decisions and they all went Wagga Wagga's way. His team won the local premiership for twelve years in succession on account of his umpiring.

The day after Freddie arrived, the grand final match was scheduled to begin, with Wagga Wagga one of the teams, needless to say in line for its thirteenth premiership in succession.

The secretary of the opposing team, a bloke named Shoofty Simpson, called a conference in the Cricketers' Arms Hotel, in Wagga Wagga's main street.

'Listen, mates,' Shoofty said to his committee members. 'We'll be robbed by McConkidale again tomorrow. There's only one thing for it: Freddie Trueman is up here on holiday, staying with that Pommy squatter out in the bush. I move we bring Trueman into our team under an assumed name – to offset the advantage of One-eyed Mick.'

The motion was carried unanimously and Shoofty was detailed to approach Freddie, who just happened to be gargling his tonsils in the next bar with his host.

Shoofty Simpson told them the story.

'Why don't you report him to the local cricket association?' Freddie suggested, with a laugh.

'No use,' replied the secretary. 'His father's the president of the association, owns half the town and is the mayor, as well.'

18

Freddie's host, the Pommy squatter, took his cricket very seriously. 'It's an utter disgrace,' he said. 'McConkidale is the World's Worst Cricket Umpire – and he just seems to give all his bad decisions in favour of Wagga Wagga.'

Then the secretary informed them about the unanimous motion carried by his committee: to wit, to bring in Freddie Trueman as a member of their team under an assumed name.

Freddie's host said: 'Something has to be done. Might be a good idea to play a joke on McConkidale.'

They drank a few beers over the problem then Freddie Trueman said: 'Right, lads, I'll play. Ooh, aye, and I'll give McConkidale a right rollicking.'

His team won the toss and sent Wagga Wagga in to bat. The captain threw the ball to Freddie 'Smith', the new bloke with the black hair and the Yorkshire accent.

Freddie measured out a short run up: no trouble bowling out bush batsmen on a concrete and matting wicket, even with a crook umpire.

One-eyed Mick McConkidale, the World's Worst Cricket Umpire, was at the bowler's end.

Freddie bowled the first ball about half pace wide outside the off stump: didn't want to make things too obvious. To his surprise the batsman reached out his bat and snicked the ball straight into the wicket-keeper's gloves.

'How's that?' asked Freddie, turning to the World's Worst Umpire.

'Not out,' was the firm reply.

Freddie hadn't quite believed all Shoofty had told him about McConkidale; thought he might have made an honest mistake. But he went back and bowled one a bit faster, his famous outswinger this time. The batsman swished it high over the slips and the third man caught it.

'Well, how's that?' Freddie asked the umpire, with a glare.

'Not out.'

So Freddie knew that Shoofty had told him nothing more than the gospel truth – and that the only way to get the batsman out was to clean bowl him.

He took a longer run up and bowled a faster ball – not full Test Match speed but fast enough for Wagga Wagga – good length, right on the middle stump. It rapped the batsman on the pads.

19

'How's that then?' Freddie yelled.

The World's Worst Umpire hesitated a trifle then shook his head: 'Not out.'

'Why? Was it going under the stumps?' Freddie Trueman asked, his features suggesting satire.

'You do your job and I'll do mine,' One-eyed Mick McConkidale snapped, by way of reply. 'I don't want any cheek from you.'

'Pity you never brought your guide dog with you,' Freddie muttered – and set off to measure out his full Test Match run up, thinking, 'I'll put one around the batsman's bloody ears.'

And he bowled a bumper, did Fred, straight at the batsman's head.

The batsman moved inside the ball and hooked it to deep fine leg. A fieldsman ran around the fence, got under the ball and caught it in full view of everyone on the ground.

The whole fielding side appealed with Freddie: 'How's that?'

'Not out!' was all One-eyed Mick McConkidale said.

'You nearly had him that time, Fred . . . '

But Freddie Trueman (alias Smith) wasn't beaten yet. He had one more card up his sleeve. Ping in a yorker, right under the bat and send the stumps flying. Then McConkidale would have to give him out.

So he went back again, ran up flat out, leapt in the air and bowled at his full speed – a hundred miles an hour.

The batsman didn't even see the ball. It landed right in his block-hole and hit the wicket. It broke the middle stump into three pieces, sent the leg stump flying into the pavilion and the off stump spinning over the sight screen.

Well, Freddie thought, that settles that. Even this character will have to give him out now.

He turned around and was just about to appeal when One-eyed Mick McConkidale said: 'Cripes, mate, that was close; you nearly had him that time.'

5

The Lord's Prayer

Fred Trueman

That great character, Emmott Robinson was Yorkshire's opening bowler and a useful batsman; that was in the days when they usually only spoke twice in the matches with Lancashire. They said, 'Good morning' and 'How's that?'

Now, the old Emmott loved to win cricket matches and would come at any kind of gamesmanship to achieve that aim.

Above all, Emmott liked to beat his old rivals, Lancashire. In those days, Yorkshire and Lancashire were the great County sides and still are, as far as I am concerned. And Emmott always arrived early for any match against Lancashire.

Well, one day, the great rival teams were to play a decisive match in the competition, so the old Emmott arrived very early indeed.

He looked in the Yorkshire dressing-room and nobody was there. He looked into the Lancashire dressing-room – nobody there. So he rushed back to the Yorkshire dressing-room, had a good look around, then grabbed one of the cushions and went into the shower room.

He knelt on the cushion and prayed: 'Dear Lord above. I know Thou art the greatest judge of any cricket match that ever takes place. Well, today, the two most powerful teams in County cricket oppose each other. Now, Lord, if Yorkshire have the best side they will win. And I suppose that, if Lancashire have the best side, they will win. If the teams are equal or if it rains heavily, the game will be drawn.

'But, Lord, if Thou will just keep out of it for the next seventy-two hours, we'll knock bloody hell out of this Lancashire lot!'

6
Famous Last Words: 'Why doesn't he take me off?'

Fred Trueman

A certain County Vice-Captain was very absent-minded.

On one occasion, he went to the wicket to face up – and didn't realize he'd left his bat in the pavilion until he tried to take guard without it.

He even went to the wrong ground for a game on two occasions.

He was a good middle-order batsman. But, as a bowler, he was just useful enough to get a short spell as a change bowler now and then.

One day, he was bowling and getting belted all around the oval. Twenty-five runs came off his first three overs.

After five overs, his figures read none for forty-five.

And they took no less than twenty runs from his sixth over.

As he went back to begin his seventh over (the longest spell of bowling he'd ever done), he said to the fieldsman at deep mid-on: 'What's wrong with the Captain? Why doesn't he take me off? I'm getting hit all over the ground.'

The fieldsman replied: 'The Captain's not playing. He's in hospital, remember? It's about time you asked yourself those questions.'

7

The Most Expensive Test Match I Ever Played In

Fred Trueman

The most unforgettable – and the most expensive – Test Match I ever played in was on the Trinidad Ground.

What marvellous people the West Indians are! Cricket is their national game – and they'll come for miles to watch it.

I used to love to play on those islands. It was always beautiful to bowl, lovely and warm. You felt loose: no muscle trouble. You always got a breeze blowing that kept you fresh.

And I won't forget that particular match in Trinidad, will I?

The north coast of Jamaica is one of the most beautiful places in the world. And I remember one morning lying on a beautiful beach, taking in the sun, sipping an ice-cold gin and tonic, watching the dusky maidens sway by on their way to market with their baskets on their heads, singing their calypsos. Thinking to myself, how do the poor in Yorkshire live?

I had seen Runaway Bay, Discovery Bay, Montego Bay. Fantastic!

And I was lying there, taking all this in when suddenly a shadow was cast across me, and I looked up and there was my captain, Peter May, and what he said to me was to shatter my whole tour.

He looked down at me, and I looked up, and he said: 'Frederick,' so I knew something was wrong. I kept things formal and replied: 'Yes, Captain, what is it?'

He said: 'I have some bad news for you.'

I said: 'What's that?'

He said: 'You are playing in the Second Test at Trinidad.'

I asked: 'Why?'

He said: 'There're only nine fit and you are one of them.'

So, I was playing in the Second Test at Trinidad – and that cost me a lot of money.

I arrived at this beautiful ground, shaped like an oval, called Queen's Park. The backcloth is superb, these beautiful hills go right up, and when the sun shines on them in a certain way you get this beautiful blue-purple sort of sheen and in the summer you get the beautiful laburnum trees in full flower – beautiful yellow against the purple on the hills.

In the corner of the ground is this big, beautiful scoreboard which makes the one at Trent Bridge look as though it's man-handled. They spell your name right. They put an 'E' in mine. And I liked that because I don't want some other bugger getting the credit.

And that Test Match in Trinidad, the West Indies will never forget it – and neither will I.

In Trinidad, to the right-hand side of the pavilion is the great long stand known as the black stand. That's where all the families come – cats, dogs, pigs, goats, the lot. All the ladies in their lovely frocks dancing, the steel bands playing. I'd love to put them in the Long Room at Lords for half an hour before a match started. Some of them old so-and-so's in that Library, they'd never come back again.

This ground at Trinidad holds 27 000 jammed full and on this Saturday there were 33 000 there and another 7000 in the trees round the ground, all voicing their opinion.

I remember that great, dear friend of mine, Sir Frank Worrell, the late Frankie Worrell, as he came in to bat during that match. Our side was doing a lap of honour at the time, having taken a wicket – the umpire had looked our way. And this black stand rose to him and the noise was fantastic, and I said to Frank: 'By God, Frankie, you've got a few supporters there.'

And Frank Worrell said: 'No, they're not my supporters, Fred, they're all yours.'

I asked: 'Well, why mine?'

And he said: 'That stand is there to remind you of York-shire and the slagheaps where you bloody come from.'

Around this black stand is where all the action took place. They were supping white rum straight out of the bottle, three-and-six a time, playing roulette, find-the-lady, dice and cards, fighting in heaps – and that was before the match started.

My troubles started before the match, too.

For some reason, a West Indian player said to me: 'We don't get the crowds we used to get.'

And I replied: 'No wonder, they're nearly all living in bloody England.'

That cost me fifty quid bonus – and the match hadn't even started.

Quite a few things went wrong that Saturday.

First thing that went wrong was that our captain, Peter May, won the toss. The second thing that went wrong: he had a flash of inspiration and we batted first on a good wicket.

It could happen to nobody else in cricketing history; it could only happen to Fred Trueman: I'd lost fifty quid good-conduct bonus before the match started – and I lost another fifty quid while England were still batting.

I was sitting in the dressing-room in my favourite position, feet up, legs crossed, smoking my pipe, suitably attired for the weather – I was just wearing my jockstrap. Sitting alongside me, my lifelong friend, Brian Statham. He was dressed exactly the same way as I was, smoking a cigarette, except his jockstrap was bigger. Then I saw one of the funniest things I've ever seen on a cricket field, possibly *the* funniest: I saw our captain, Peter May, batting.

And I saw him hit a straight six into a palm tree and fourteen West Indians fell out.

Now, I've got a funny sense of humour, and that cost me another fifty quid.

All I said was: 'What an advert for Rowntree's chocolate drops.' And they fined me on the spot.

The third thing that went wrong was we declared at 687 for seven.

So me and my old mate, Brian, we put the overalls on, didn't we.

We walked through their Long Room, down the steps and Brian had his arm round me. And I looked at him and I said: 'Brian, you're looking very worried.'

And he said: 'I am.'

And I said: 'What for, we've 687 on the board; the last time this happened was at the Oval in 1938.'

He said: 'I couldn't care a bugger, *we* weren't playing.'

I asked: 'Well, what's worrying you?'

He said: 'I'll tell you. You and I, we haven't batted.'

Because we had a law, Brian Statham and I: them that bat on it, bowl on it. But nobody took any notice of us.

I said: 'Come on, stop worrying, we shall do this lot. We'll get stuck into these West Indians and we'll knock seven different colours out of them. We'll hit 'em with everything bar the pavilion and the umpire. We'll bruise this lot as white as what we are, before we're finished.'

So he said: 'Okay, you're on. Have I got a choice of ends?'

I said: 'Yes, downhill into the wind.'

Now, people used to say to me, 'Why is it I always bowled with the wind?' Well, with beans and rice for two and half months you haven't got much choice, have you?

The real reason was Brian Statham was thinner than me and he cut through the wind better.

So I said: 'Come on, Brian, we'll have a right go at these West Indians.'

We gave them some stick that afternoon, didn't we?

At quarter to four, they were 183 for one, and the wicket was a doubtful run-out that caused a riot. (I actually should have had one of them leg before wicket - but getting an l.b.w. decision out of a West Indian umpire is like trying to plait sawdust.)

Anyway, at 210 for one, Peter May says to me: 'Frederick,' he says.

And I said: 'Yes, Captain, what is it?'

He says: 'I think we'll change the bowling.'

I said: 'Has he at the other end agreed?'

Peter said: 'Yes.'

So I said: 'Well, I agree': there was no way that Brian Statham could bowl when I wasn't, because he might get wickets and we'd not have been level.

So I said: 'Okay,' and the bowling was changed, so Brian Statham bowled uphill and I bowled downhill. So at 225 for one, I said to Peter May: 'Captain!'

He said: 'Yes, Frederick, what is it?'

I said: 'I've got an idea.'

And he said: 'Good, what is it?'

So I said: 'This little fellow here at this end, Basil Butcher, have you noticed anything about him?'

Peter May replied: 'Yes, he's black.'

So I thought to myself: Frederick, there is somebody on this field not thinking, and it's not you.

Peter May then asked: 'What have you noticed?'

I said: 'I think I can get him out.'

Peter said: 'Good, we've been trying to get him out since a quarter to eleven this morning.'

I said: 'Captain, I think I can do it. Have you noticed he's about five feet three tall. Watch him when he plays a cut shot outside the offstump – he's bowlegged, and he bends his legs even further still, and when he actually makes contact with the ball he's about four feet ten. Even on beans and rice I think I can get one that high.'

Peter May asked: 'What do you suggest?'

I said: 'Three slips.'

He said: 'I'll telephone them.'

So messages were sent and eventually three slips arrived prompted by the Bradford lad who was playing for England, Raman Subba Row. He was the only one who had understood the smoke signals to bring them in.

So the three slips arrived. Now Raman Subba Row was on a trip, I think, to add colour to the batting side. So they arrived, all three of them, all from university. From Oxford University at first slip: Sir Colin Cowdrey (that's if Ted Heath gets back in). At second slip: from Cambridge University the old Bradford lad himself, Raman Subba Row. At third slip, also from Cambridge University, Lord Edward Dexter – he was there, too. And Peter May, he's gone to gully; well, he's the Captain, he can please himself where he goes.

And he said: 'Well, are you ready, Frederick?'

I said: 'Yes.'

At cover I've got Geoff Pullar of Lancashire, so you can tell how hard up we were for fielders, for a start.

I've got my old mate, Brian Statham, at mid-wicket. The rest of the lads are scattered around the field somewhere. We hadn't seen Ray Illingworth for three weeks; not since he got none for 148 in Jamaica.

Anyway, I'm there, left sleeve rolled up, shoulder into the wind, and away I go. And I smash this ball in outside the off stump with everything I've got. And it bounced, and he's there, is Basil Butcher indeed. The old legs are bent and he goes for the cut. And he gets a beautiful top edge, straight to Raman Subba Row at second slip. I'm up in the air: this is my Test wicket, it's nothing to do with Peter May, I've thought this out.

I'm full of jubilation, the ball speeding to Raman and I'm thinking, Fred, another Test wicket, it's yours lad.

And I'm there congratulating myself, and Raman's there, and his eyes are getting wider, and this ball's hurtling at him.

And you know how the slips get down with their backsides in the air. This ball went straight to Raman Subba Row and he never got a touch. He never laid a finger on that catch.

The ball went straight through his legs, it missed 'em, and it went for four runs. I stood at the end of my follow-through, one hand on hip, trying to look diplomatic. He looked at me and I looked straight at him.

I daren't say a word, I only had fifty quid bonus left! And I had to try and prove to the wife that I'd been *somewhere* for three months.

No third man, and four runs. So I stood there and eventually the ball came back from the crowd, and it was thrown to me and I (very cleverly, I thought) caught it with one hand. Walking back, I looked at the ball, and this is when I realized that the West Indies know their cricket. That ball had been in the crowd only about two minutes and there were four razor blade cuts in it.

Walking back to the end of my run-up, I still daren't say a word, only eleven of us and about 33 000 of them and some reserves. And I walked back, polishing the ball like I usually do, on my trousers, you know, right hand for swing and, being Jewish, left hand for a bit of pleasure. And I finished the over with no further incident taking place.

And I stood at the end of my follow-through, both hands on hips, trying to look more diplomatic than before, watching the field as it changed over.

The slips were coming down and Raman Subba Row got to about three or four yards from me, and he circled me and I watched him as he went by and he looked at me, walked straight on without missing a step, and he suddenly spoke from the corner of his mouth and said: 'Sorry, Fred, didn't get a touch.'

Trying to look diplomatic

I said: 'Yes, I noticed,' or words to that effect. 'What about the four runs?'

And he said: 'I'm sorry about that, it might have been better if I'd kept my legs together.'

So I said: 'It's a pity your mother didn't.'

When I got back to England the following April, I owed the MCC a hundred and two quid!

8
Bloody Beauty!

Frank Hardy

This story comes from Neil Hawke, former Australian Test all-rounder, who now lives in Lancashire.

Neil says he heard Wally Grout, who used to bend bananas up in Queensland and kept wicket for Australia in his spare time, tell it at a cocktail party years ago in Australia.

Wally claimed to have heard it from Bill Tallon. Bill's main claim to fame was that he was a brother of Don Tallon, the great Australian wicket-keeper. The Tallons were also banana benders. Wally Grout succeeded Don as Queensland and Australia wicket-keeper.

Bill Tallon himself played a few seasons for Queensland as a medium-paced bowler. He didn't leave any figures in the record books but he had one day of glory on the Gabba Cricket Ground when he opened the bowling for Queensland against South Australia.

Here is how Bill Tallon told the story.

'There I was opening the bowling. I've got the new ball and I'm running in to bowl the first ball to a bloke named Nietzsche, a left-hander. Bloody good bat. It was an in-swinger and he got an outside edge.

'Bloody beauty! Me brother, Don, caught it in front of first slip.

'One for none!

'So out came Badcock. He was a bloody good bat, too, but I had the new ball and I could swing it a bit. So I ran up and bowled to Badcock and, all of a sudden, he went for the cover drive and got a thick edge.

'Bloody beauty! Me brother Don caught it in front of second slip.

'Two for none!

'So out came the great Don Bradman. I felt a bit nervous: I'd never bowled to Bradman before. But I had the new ball. And there I was bowling to Don Bradman himself. I'm swinging the ball both ways and getting a bit of bounce; when, all of a sudden, I dropped one short and he went for the hook. He hit it so high that fine leg ran for it, square leg ran for it, mid-on ran for it, I ran for it meself and I got a sunburnt mouth waiting for it to come down.

'Bloody beauty. Me brother, Don, got under the ball first and caught it.

'Three for 284!'

9
Famous Last Words: 'He won't get me out again'

Fred Trueman

Your really top-class batsman can play any type of bowling and no one bowler can get the mocker on him (as Denis Lillee did with a certain English batsman).

But there are many really good, first-class batsmen who cannot play a certain type of bowling, a certain bowler even.

Denis Smith was a good left-hand batsman in the thirties, but he couldn't pick Tich Freeman's googly – though, let's face it, Tich did bowl a beautiful wrong 'un.

One day, Denis went to face Tich Freeman. Before departing from the pavilion he told his team mates that he would get Tich Freeman's measure, if it was the last thing he did.

But, needless to say, he failed to pick the googly and was out cheaply.

Returning to the pavilion, he announced: 'He won't get me out again. Next time, I'll hit his leg break out of the ground – if it isn't a googly.'

10
A Shaggy Cricket Story

Frank Hardy

A few years ago, in Australia, there was a boom in pub cricket. The drinkers at one hotel in a suburb or town would challenge the drinkers at another hotel to a friendly game. The publicans would supply two or three eighteen-gallon kegs of beer and a good time would be had by all.

Of course, the quality of the cricket would decline as the wits came out and the day wore on. These games were usually played on a Sunday: the better the day, the better the deed.

Melbourne Cup Day was also a favourite occasion for pub cricket matches, Australia being the only country in the world where there is a national public holiday for a horse race. In fact, this particular match which has gone down in history was actually played on Melbourne Cup Day, 1963, in a place called Boraloolla. That day, the crowd got free beer, a free cricket match, a bet on the Cup – and they saw the Eighth Wonder of the World.

There was the usual argument about the most effective way to open a keg without the beer going flat, because most Australians are authorities on opening kegs; and then, after a few grogs to see them go, the captains tossed and the revelry was about to begin.

The umpires were ready to go on to the field, each with a jug of beer in hand to improve his vision so he could give decisions to his own team without fear or favour.

The star of the visiting team, an opening batsman, was also ready; he wore one batting glove (on the wrong hand); one of his pads was white, the other tan; his trousers were navy blue and he wore a tee-shirt labelled BEER IS A

FOOD – and a digger's hat. His bat was split and repaired with string dipped in tar.

Two drunks, after a long struggle, had managed to peg down the matting on the asphalt wicket. They then proceeded to put the stumps in, discovered there were only five – and substituted a piece of a branch from a wattle tree with yellow blooms on top of it.

The game was about to proceed when the visiting captain did a slow head count to make sure his team were all present. Only ten men. He double checked. Only ten bloody men.

The captain called on his team to line up. 'There's some bastard missing.'

They lined up rather unsteadily (the bar had been open for two hours). 'We can beat them with a man short,' some smart Alec said.

'Not without Sammy Smith, one of our opening batsmen, we can't,' the captain said. 'Sammy's definitely not here.'

One of the drunks who had helped put the matting down quipped: 'If Sammy's not here, he must be dead. He wouldn't miss a day of free beer. We'd better send around the hat.'

The visiting captain approached the Boraloolla committee and politely sought a replacement. The Boraloolla mob weren't keen to help out: they'd wagered heavily on the local team.

At last, an old bloke sitting in a cart under a near-by tree, called to the visiting captain: 'Maybe I can help you, mate!'

The captain walked over, a trifle unsteadily, had a look at the old fellow: getting on for eighty, about a dollar's worth of clothes on, corks in his hat and as skinny as a flagpole – would weigh about five stone wringing wet in an army overcoat with housebricks in the pockets.

He'd be useless, the captain decided, and asked, his features suggesting sarcasm and a fondness for beer: 'Fancy yourself as a cricketer, do you, mate?'

'No,' the old bloke replied. 'Never played the game in me life – but my horse is the best opening bat in Queensland.'

'Is he now?' the captain said and, being half pissed and ready for a joke, asked the Boraloolla mob if he could bring in a horse as a replacement for Sammy Smith.

Well, citizens of Boraloolla are all characters (no people there, only characters) so they had a conference around the kegs and agreed: better to have a horse than a ring-in batsman who could play, which they suspected the visitors might be ready to come at.

By this time, the old bloke had unyoked his horse and approached the assembled cricketers.

'Hang on a minute,' he said. 'There's a few conditions attached to this. My horse here is an opening bat, the best in all bloody Queensland, so he will insist on opening the innings and facing the bowling, taking the first over.'

So it was agreed.

'And another thing, he'll want four pads: can't risk him getting injured in a picnic game.'

Well, by this time everybody is laughing their heads off – especially the Boraloolla mob. But the laugh was on the other side of their faces when they tried to scrape up four pads for the horse. The·teams had only five pads between them and, as the old bloke was adamant on the horse wearing four of them, the star opening batsman had to surrender his white pad and was left with the tan one – on his wrong leg.

Word went around the town that the Eighth Wonder of the World was about to be seen in Boraloolla – a horse opening the innings in a cricket match on Melbourne Cup Day! So the crowd swelled until six more kegs of beer had to be sent for.

At last, the two openers went to the wicket, amid ribald cheers from the well-oiled throats of the spectators.

The horse took guard – and promptly hit the first ball straight out of the ground for six.

The Boraloolla crowd couldn't believe their eyes, especially when the horse cover drove the second ball for four – cracked the third and fourth balls for six, the fifth for four – and the last ball of the most expensive over ever bowled in Boraloolla for another six.

The star opening batsman faced the second over. He was in form and wanted to get the bowling for himself, so he played down the line until the fifth ball when he called the horse for a single.

But the horse just stood there, leaning on his bat.

When he saw the horse was refusing to run, the star batsman turned and ran back. He nearly got run out.

He scowled at· the horse, placed the next ball for an easy

single and called again – but the horse didn't move. The star bat went back again and threw himself flat to just scramble home.

He got up, dusted his clothes, went down the wicket to the horse and he said: 'Listen, why didn't you run?'

'Run!' the horse replied. 'If I could run I wouldn't be here playing in a pub cricket match with a mug like you, I'd be down at Flemington racing in the Melbourne bloody Cup.'

If you don't believe this story you can check the records which show that an eight-year-old gelding made a century against Boraloolla on Melbourne Cup Day, 1963.

11

The Hard-Hitting Batsman from the Yorkshire Dales

Fred Trueman

In the Yorkshire dales, many years ago, in a small competition, a hard-hitting batsman, the local blacksmith, was belting the visiting bowlers all over the ground.

He were a right bugger, weren't he: cross bat, unorthodox stance, an eye like a hawk and powerful wrists. He were giving them a right rollicking, I can tell you; made 80 in the first hour.

He was very strong on the leg side and had lost two balls in a turnip patch just outside the square-leg boundary of the small oval.

The visiting Captain got desperate after this big-hitter had passed the century mark – and lost another ball amongst the turnips. So this Captain called the Vice-Captain and the bowler aside for a conference.

The Captain said: 'Listen, we've got to get this bloke out somehow, or, at least, cut the scoring rate. I suggest we bowl outside the off stump.'

The Vice-Captain said: 'That suits me: I'm tired of chasing the ball into that turnip patch.'

The bowler said: 'Yes,' but then he had to, didn't he?

So he put one down wide outside the off stump but, you wouldn't want to know, the big-hitting batsman stepped across and pulled it around to square leg.

It went fast towards the boundary.

The Vice-Captain ran around to try to cut it off.

A spectator yelled: 'He can't stop it!'

The Captain said: 'He has stopped it. Well fielded!'

The Vice-Captain turned for the throw in.

The hard-hitting batsman wasn't the fastest of runners, being built like a brick chicken-house.

The Vice-Captain hurled a mighty throw – and scattered the stumps at the bowler's end.

The blacksmith was a yard out of his ground.

The umpire said: 'Out!'

The Captain ran over to the Vice-Captain and shook his hand. 'I'm glad to see the last of him. That was a great throw.'

'Ooh, aye,' the Vice-Captain replied. 'But you better give me a hand to find the ball – that were a turnip I ran him out with.'

12

Famous Last Words:
'I'm the best judge of a single'
Fred Trueman

Cyril Washbrook and Alan Wharton, famous Lancashire opening batsmen, didn't see eye to eye, as the saying goes. They made a lot of runs together. But they didn't get along too well, otherwise, did they?

One day, they opened the innings as usual, got going and were still not out at lunch.

In the afternoon when Washbrook was on 90 and Wharton 99 Cyril pushed one towards mid-wicket, called for a quick single and set off.

But Alan refused to budge, put up his hand and yelled: 'Go back!'

Cyril stopped dead in his tracks, dived back, flung himself flat on his belly with his bat outstretched – and just scrambled home to prevent the run out.

Picking himself up, Cyril Washbrook observed the green and brown patches on his knees, belly and elbows, dusted himself off and walked down the wicket.

Cyril Washbrook said vehemently: 'It is a well-known fact that I am the best judge of a single in all England.'

Alan Wharton replied calmly: 'And it's a well-known fact that, when I'm on 99, I'm the best judge of a run in all the bloody world.'

13
The Headmaster Who Loved Cricket
Fred Trueman

One of the greatest cricket lovers I ever met was the head-master of a public school. I met him when I went to his school to try to teach the students something about the art of cricket.

Because I feel that I owe the great game of cricket a lot, I often go to different schools – public schools, comprehensive schools, state schools, council schools. The sporting facilities at the state and council schools and even at some of the comprehensive schools are appalling. I've seen schools where they play no soccer, no rugby, no cricket even – because they haven't the facilities.

We claim to be a sporting nation. We acclaim anyone who brings back a medal from the Olympics. If England win the Ashes, the hangers-on are there to say: 'What a wonderful performance!' But we never get down to providing facilities for our future stars in the schools.

The public schools usually have every sporting facility: rugby grounds, athletic fields, cricket fields. The lot.

Well, first time I met this old headmaster, I found that his school had excellent facilities – especially for cricket. He was a cricket fanatic.

'Thank you for coming, Fred,' he said. 'I know a man who was born next door to you.' (I didn't tell him that I'd met a thousand men who claimed to have been born next door to me.)

A couple of the kids took my gear and called me Sir. They were great lads. I trained them well over the years – they're supping pints of ale like veterans.

Last year this headmaster told me that his first-year

players had won fourteen matches in succession; no losses, no draws, all outright wins. He was so proud he sat up for two nights and went through 104 years of the school score books – and found that his lads had created an all-time record.

So he called the parents together and told them the story: 'These lads must be rewarded.'

And they said: 'What have you got in mind, headmaster?'

And he replied: 'Well, I've taken the liberty of organizing an educational trip to Paris.'

The parents said: 'Aye' – and they dipped in the old back

One of a thousand

pockets, and pulled out fifty notes each (the old tax evasion, you know).

Well, what a trip! The Eiffel Tower, Napoleon's Tomb, Notre Dame, the Crazy Horse, the Left Bank, the lot!

On the last day, the old headmaster got the lads together, didn't he, and he said: 'Lads, I've got some wonderful news for you. The night life in Paris is the most wonderful in the world. I can't let you leave without seeing it. And you are very lucky because the French educational authorities have arranged for you to go to a famous night club at the top of the Pigalle.'

The lads couldn't wait. Upstairs they went – brilliantine on the hair, creases in the trousers; the bus was due to leave at eight o'clock, they were ready at seven.

So they get there and sit in the front row sipping watered-down champagne. And the headmaster was thinking: what a wonderful thing for them.

The lights dim, there was a roll of drums and the beautiful stage lit up with all the coloured lights. Another roll of drums and the stage was enveloped in velvet curtains.

And the headmaster thought: what wonderful technology. What an education for these boys.

Then the band played and the curtains rolled back – and twenty-four beautiful ladies came on dressed only in ostrich feathers, kicking their legs in time with the music.

And the lads were not missing a kick!

And the headmaster thought: a stroke of inspiration for me to think of this. Well, the lads deserve it: they did so well at cricket.

Suddenly, a fanfare of trumpets and a man jumped from behind the curtain: silk topper, white cravat, long-tail evening suit, patent leather shoes, white gloves, and black stick with silver knob. As the music played, he flicked the stick here, there and everywhere. And as he flicked it, the ostrich feathers fell off the girls, one at a time, didn't they? Until there were twenty-four ladies on the stage – as naked as the day they were born.

And those little lads watched from the front row, with wide eyes.

And the headmaster thought: good God, they didn't tell me this would happen.

He's in a bit of a sweat, is the old headmaster, when suddenly there was a tap on his shoulder.

It was one of the boys, and so he turns and says: 'Yes, George-Brown-George, what is it?'

George-Brown-George says: 'Permission to speak, Sir.'

'Granted. What is it?'

'It's young Greenes-Mead, Sir.'

'What about him?'

And young George-Brown-George replies: 'Well, Sir, his mother told him that if he ever saw anything like this, he'd turn to stone. And he thinks he's just started.'

14
Blood on the Wicket

Fred Trueman

Fast bowlers are a rare breed of people – and there are three different kinds.

There is the easy-going, gentle bowler who can bowl quick; there is the temperamental bowler who can bowl quick; and there is the dangerous bowler who can bowl quick and, for some unknown reason, likes to hit batsmen, derives pleasure from injuring batsmen.

I've been blamed for trying to hit batsmen. A batsman actually said to me one day: 'You tried to maim me today, Trueman.'

'No, I didn't,' I said. 'If I laid you out and couldn't bowl at you again, I couldn't get your wicket. And I'd rather get you out than hurt you.'

I never wanted to hit or maim a batsman. It's not in my character. I could not have gone through life if, for instance, I had hit a man with a new ball and blinded him for life. I couldn't live with it: knowing I had done a thing like that on purpose.

But there are some fast bowlers who seem to like to hit batsmen. In fact, one of them was quoted as saying: 'I like to see blood on the wicket.'

One day, in a County match, one of these 'blood on the wicket' fast bowlers was playing on a pitch that suited his pace and bounce and movement.

He saw a likely victim in a man who batted number four in the opposing side.

Wickets had fallen and this batsman came in and took guard. A big man, about eighteen stone; walked with his feet at a quarter past nine. He had an awkward stance; legs rigid,

' Umpire called wide '

DAVID
LANGDON

bat away from his body. His backside stuck out so far, as he leaned down to hold the bat, that once when he had been hit on the rump the umpire had called wide.

This batsman was a forward player and not equipped to contend with a really fast bowler with conditions to suit.

So this fast bowler thinks to himself: 'Here's one I can take the mickey out of. I'll give this big bloke a right rollicking, play a symphony on his ribs and a rock and roll number on his thick head.'

He didn't think of taking his wicket, did he? Not this 'blood on the wicket' bowler. He just wanted to embarrass him and hurt him. And, of course, the batsman being only a front-foot player, it was easy for a bowler with exceptional pace to hit him.

Well, up runs the fast bowler and the first ball hit the big fella under the heart – and down went the big frame on to the ground.

The fieldsmen gathered around. 'Are you all right?' one of them asked. But the bowler just went back to his mark, thinking, 'I can get this bloke out when I want to; meanwhile I'll play a tune on him.'

Well, the batsman got up, rubbing his heart and took guard again. He didn't have a lot of ability but he had a heart as big as a dustbin lid.

He tried to get behind the next ball and it struck him a painful blow on the arm. Then the demon bowler ripped one in off the seam that hit him on the 'box' - and down he went again in great agony.

A sympathetic fielder suggested: 'Don't rub, count.'

Well, up he got again and, in the next over this fast bowler kept hitting him: on the arm, on the shoulder, on the chest - but he kept coming back for more and getting the odd run as he went along.

In his fifth over, the fast bowler really dug one in. The batsman couldn't get out of the way and it struck him on the head, and he went down on the ground again - this time out cold.

The fieldsmen and the crowd were apprehensive: was he seriously injured? When he came to, the twelfth man gave him two aspirin tablets and a glass of water. He got those into himself and staggered to his feet. He had a lump on his head as big as a turnip but said he was fit to bat on.

The demon bowler went back to his run up thinking, I've got him intimidated, now I'll bowl him out.

He was just running up when the batsman put up his hand and said: 'Stop!'

The umpire was worried: 'What's the matter? Do you feel sick?'

The batsman replied: 'No, but pardon me for a minute. Do you think I could have the sight board moved?'

'Certainly,' said the umpire. 'Where would you like it?'

'Well,' replied the batsman, who wasn't as silly as he looked and turned out to have a sharp sense of humour, 'the way he's bowling, preferably in the middle of the wicket.'

And he had the last laugh, didn't he, as things turned out: in between being hit, he took fifty runs, mainly off the fast bowler, under conditions where the whole team might have been out for fifty. Eventually, one of the spinners got him out.

As he walked back to the pavilion, he said to the 'blood on the wicket' bowler: 'You gave me fifty bruises but I took fifty runs, mainly off you. So I've come out on top.'

'I could have got you out in the first over,' the demon bowler snarled.

'Probably you could have,' the batsman replied, rubbing his sore head, as he raised his cap to the applause of the crowd. 'But you were more interested in hitting me than in getting me out.'

He walked away a few yards, then came back to the fast bowler and said, as an afterthought: 'There's one thing I'll say for you.'

'What's that?'

'You're never likely to suffer from meningitis.'

'Why?'

'Because that is a brain disease.'

15

Famous Last Words: 'You wouldn't give me out for that, would you?'

Frank Hardy

One of the great characters of post-war cricket was the Australian opening batsman, Sid Barnes, popularly known as Barnsey. A controversial figure throughout his career, Barnsey was finally made twelfth man for New South Wales against South Australia at the Adelaide Cricket Ground.

To show his displeasure, Barnsey came on to the field with the drinks – replete with clothes brush, hair spray and other accoutrements not considered strictly essential and proceeded to administer to the fieldsmen.

The crowd were delighted – but the Board of Control were not amused and mooted disciplinary action. Sid Barnes 'got in first' and announced his retirement.

Barnsey had had a bad babit of arguing with umpires, often successfully, but he met his match in the shape of Alec Skelding, famous English umpire and a noted wit.

One day at Northampton, Alec Skelding gave Sid Barnes out leg before to the bowling of Bert Nutter.

In fact, before Alec could raise his hand, Barnsey hastened to ask: 'You wouldn't give me out for that, would you?'

Alec raised his finger and said: 'Out – and I don't want any cheek from you.'

Still at the crease, Sid asked: 'Where's your dark glasses?'

'Walk,' said Alec Skelding.

Barnsey persisted: 'Where's your white stick?'

'Walk, I told yer,' Alec said.

'Well, where's your guide dog?' Barnsey asked.

'I got rid of him,' retorted Alec Skelding finally. 'Same as I'm getting rid of thee – for yapping too much. So bugger off!'

16

The Inseparable Opening Batsmen

Frank Hardy

Herbert and Harry, batsmen for the County were called the Inseparable Opening Batsmen, because they were hard to separate when batting and even harder to separate off the field.

They had been born in the same year, went to the same school and shared the same desk. They each had a bat in their hand before they were six years old – and were soon playing for the junior school team.

Their parents realized that their cricket talents, with proper nurturing, would lead them to green pastures. So the lads went to the County nets on the same day, got their County caps together and played their first match on the same day. They were soon opening the innings and had perfect understanding between the wickets.

They went everywhere together: drinks at the pub, Saturday night dances. And, where the fairer sex were involved, they went out as a foursome.

They always roomed together when their side was playing away from home – and this was where the only discord entered their lives.

Herbert had a bad habit of talking and walking in his sleep.

Sometimes he would sit bolt upright and yell out: 'How is he?' or, 'Well caught, Harry' or, 'There's one in it, Harry' or, 'Good shot, Harry.'

This disturbed Harry's sleep but he didn't complain too much. But the sleep-walking was a more serious problem: Herbert began to walk in his sleep regularly when they shared a hotel room together. He would get up, wander into the corridor or on to the balcony – and Harry would stay awake so he could rescue him from danger.

On one occasion, Harry had to restrain Herbert from peeing in the cupboard drawer where their creams were stored.

Because of their friendship, Harry had to grin and bear it; until, one night after the last match of the season, he saw Herbert get up, kneel by the bed and start praying.

Harry listened and Herbert prayed: 'Dear Lord, above, I got your message. Thank you, Lord. I have seen the light.'

Harry got out of bed, took Herbert by the arm and said: 'You are only sleep walking, old pal; come on, now, back to bed with you.'

Herbert said: 'I'm not asleep. Never more wide awake in my life. I have seen the light in a vision – and will dedicate my life to the Lord, from now on.'

And he got back into bed, without the usual assistance from Harry and fell into an innocent sleep, like that of a child.

Next morning, at breakfast, Harry tried to pass the inci-

A more serious problem

dent off as just another sleepwalking episode – but Herbert was adamant that he had seen the light.

Well, Harry was a trifle upset but, as neither of them had been to church since their school days, convinced himself that it was just a passing phase.

But, as the winter wore on, he soon realized that his pal was in deadly earnest.

First thing that happened: Herbert gave up drinking beer. 'I'm not going to the local,' he told Harry. 'It's a den of iniquity.'

Then, when Harry suggested a night out with their current girl friends, Herbert said: 'And there'll be no more of that: sex outside of wedlock is an insult to the Lord.'

Harry was appalled: 'But what about Rosie and Rita at Bristol, Susie and Shirley in London, Molly and Polly in Bradford, Fiona and Fanny in Swansea? Who's going to tell them?'

'You can tell them,' said Herbert. 'Tell them I've seen the light, had a vision of the Lord.'

Then there was the slight problem of the racing greyhound they trained together. One Sunday it was Herbert's turn to walk the dog. Instead, he took it to church and tethered it to the hatstand in the foyer. But the vicar objected so he sold the greyhound, for half its value.

When Harry complained, Herbert said: 'We are better off without the animal. Dog racing and gambling are an abomination in the sight of the Lord.'

Well, imagine how Harry felt: he'd lost his drinking companion and his greyhound in the same month.

Worse was to follow before the winter was over. Herbert announced that he had organized a cricketers' service at the church, that he would be reading the lesson – and he expected his team mates to be present.

So Harry and a few other cricketers came along to hear Herbert open the innings for his new team. They sat in the front pews.

'Dear Brothers,' Herbert began.

Some of his team mates sniggered behind their hands until Harry glared at them.

Herbert had chosen the story of David and Goliath. 'And there went out the champion of the Philistines, named

Goliath, of Gath, whose height was six cubits and a span.'

'Nearly as big as Ken Farnes,' one cricketer whispered. 'What's a span?' another asked, but Herbert ignored him and continued.

'And his spearhead weighed six hundred shekels of iron...and he stood and he cried unto the armies of Israel... "choose you a man...if he be able to fight with me, and to kill me, then we will be your servants..." '

Well, the cricketers listened while Goliath slew a few Israelites. Then David, the little bloke, decided to have a go.

'...and choose for himself five smooth stones out of a brook, and put them in a shepherd's bag...'

By this time, the cricketers in the front pews were all ears. They were not unaware of Herbert's past life and found his transformation hard to take - but this was a good story and he was telling it well.

Herbert was also getting carried away and adding some suspenseful touches of his own.

'...and David took thence a stone and put it in the sling and whirled it around and around above his head. And Goliath was splitting his sides laughing. Then David let the stone fly, and it flew, and flew...'

One of the cricketers couldn't stand the tension any longer. He yelled out: 'Did it hit the big bloke, Herbert? Did it hit him?'

Momentarily, Herbert reverted to type: 'According to the Bible, the Holy Book, it not only hit him, it killed the big bastard stone dead.'

Well, Harry didn't forget to rub it in to Herbert about his lapse, but Herbert said: 'I prayed to the Lord and he has forgiven me.'

As the cricket season approached, Harry began to worry that Herbert might give up cricket, as well, but he came to the nets as usual and made himself available for selection in the first match.

And they were selected, of course, and padded up to open the innings when their captain won the toss.

Some of the lads ragged Herbert. One of them asked: 'Did you pray to the Lord for a big score?'

Herbert replied calmly: 'If it is the Lord's will, I'll make a century today. I've seen the light.'

As they walked onto the field, Herbert said: 'you can take the first over. You always do, and the Lord wills that I should not be selfish and take from people what is rightly theirs.'

Well, it was a dull hazy day and the new ball would swing about a lot, so Harry wished the Lord had suggested that Herbert should face up. There was an England fast bowler in the opposing team.

The first ball swung away, just outside the off stump and Harry was lucky: he played at it and just missed. In fact, he played and missed the first three balls, then fluked a single off an inside edge.

He went down the wicket and said to Herbert: 'The ball is swinging and bouncing. . .'

'The Lord will look after his own,' Herbert reassured him - and promptly hit the first ball he received over the bowler's head for six. And he hit another six off the last ball of the over.

As the field changed, Harry said to Herbert: 'Steady down, lad, we've got all day.'

Herbert said: 'The Lord looks after those who have seen the light.'

Harry didn't see the first ball of the next over and fluked another single off the second.

Herbert promptly scored two fours and two sixes - and Harry thought, he's seen the light, all right.

So Harry walked down the pitch and said to Herbert: 'Listen, old mate, I'm not seeing them too well. Would you ask the Lord to shine some of that bloody light down my end?'

17
'For God's sake, call!'

Fred Trueman

That great lad, Bomber Wells, played for Gloucester. The old Bomber was no better with the bat than Mick Cowan of Yorkshire, but he made up for it by bowling well - and having a keen sense of humour.

Bomber always came in number eleven, and only brought a bat with him because he thought it was compulsory.

Well, one day, his captain, George Emmett had batted right through and Bomber came in to join him at number eleven.

And George Emmett said: 'Give me the bowling if you can. Try to get a single off the first ball. Just push forward with a straight bat.'

Bomber said: 'Yes, Captain.'

And he pushed forward on the off side at the first ball, and it turned out quite accidentally to be a good cover drive. And it went through a gap between two fieldsmen.

Bomber Wells ran about three yards, then suddenly realized that it was him who had played it. And he couldn't believe it. He had never done anything like that before.

So he stopped and he watched the ball in admiration - then walked back to his crease.

Meanwhile, George Emmett had set off for a run. He was coming like a rocket, when he saw Bomber walk back.

So George Emmett suddenly stopped, turned around, ran about ten yards and, when he saw a fieldsman throwing the ball at the wicket at his end, dived full length.

George just made his ground before the wicket was thrown down. He got up and was covered in muck and sand from his boots to his hair.

Well, he dusted himself down.

And Bomber Wells was still standing at the crease repeating the shot at an imaginary ball, full of admiration for his effort.

And George Emmett said: 'Bomber! Come here!'

So Bomber went up to him: 'Yes, Captain, what is it?'

And George said: 'In future, when you play a shot in front of the wicket, for God's sake, call!'

And Bomber said: 'Heads!'

18

Famous Last Words: 'A case of bad captaincy'

Frank Hardy

The late Arthur Mailey, famous Aussie spin bowler between the wars, was never short of a wise-crack – even on that occasion in December 1926, when he had the misfortune to be bowling for New South Wales when Victoria made 1107, the world record score ever in any class of cricket.

On the Melbourne Cricket Ground, it was. Bill Ponsford made 352 and Jack Ryder 295. A man named Morton was run out for a duck in the middle of that innings.

Arthur Mailey finished up with 4 for 362 (or 362 for 4, in English parlance).

The newspaper men didn't forget to rub it in when they interviewed Arthur after the match.

'You've got to take into account that I had three catches dropped in the Members' Stand,' Arthur said with a grin.

The journalists weren't very impressed, so he added: 'It was a case of bad captaincy: I was just striking a length when he took me off.'

19

The Retired Yorkshire Cricketers

Fred Trueman

A cricketer can beat bad luck and bad weather, he can beat the record books – but one thing he can't beat is time.

Age conquers every sportsman in the end. The eyesight starts to fade a bit, the reflexes start to slow up – and he has to face the fact that he will soon have to retire.

Retire before the age of forty? Ooh, aye, that's how it is with a cricketer, usually. Most people can earn a living in their chosen job until sixty-five; most cricketers are finished at forty.

Very few cricketers have been lucky enough to earn their living from cricket as coach, writer, commentator or lecturer, years after retiring.

So the biggest worry a County cricketer has is what he will do when he is too old to live as a cricketer.

Take the case of the two Yorkshire cricketers who retired years ago – and couldn't find alternative employment.

George and Alf were their names.

They'd gone to school together, worked in the pits together, started playing cricket together, got their Yorkshire caps together, roomed together when the team was on tour – and retired together.

Then they started the fruitless task of trying to find a job – together.

At first, they had big ideas, didn't they? Went looking for jobs in public relations and TV advertising but they just weren't cut out for that type of work.

They gradually lowered their sights until they applied for work back in the coal mine, but nothing doing there either.

Then they applied for work cutting down willow trees for a

cricket-bat manufacturer (many a cricketer has done that in the winter or after retiring), thinking: this way at least we still make a living out of cricket, if you look at it right.

The bat manufacturer didn't doubt that they had once been able to skilfully wield a bat as cricketers but he doubted that they could wield an axe well enough to cut willow to make bats for cricketers.

So George said: 'You know, choom, we're going to have to find a job soon – no matter what it is.'

Alf replied: 'Ooh, aye, we do and all. Eighteen months it be since we retired and the benefit money all gone.'

In case people doubt the truth of this story, they should think about what happened to many old Yorkshire players in the past.

Take the case of John Thewles, who played for Yorkshire from its first County match against Notts until he retired in 1880. A journalist went looking for forgotten old players and, regarding John Thewles, received the reply: 'Think dead, if not Manchester.'

But Thewles was found trudging on foot carrying a heavy basket of laundry on his shoulder from Failsworth to Manchester, a distance of four miles; on the return journey he earned a few more pennies by carrying a load of coal.

And he was seventy years of age at the time.

He had earned his living this way since his Yorkshire benefit of £350 had been all spent, twenty years before.

Or the case of another Yorkshireman, George Pinder, the Prince of Wicket-Keepers, who also finished up living in poverty, after retiring to work in the Hickleton Main Colliery.

George wrote a letter about what 'we old players have done with our money' explaining that he earned £120 a season – and had to pay his own hotel bills and railway fares, and keep a wife and four kids. He played five months of the year and somehow survived the other seven.

George continued pathetically: 'Gentlemen who used to treat me when I was playing pass me by. They remark, "That used to be the best wicket keeper in England; poor bugger, he has spent all his money..." It's not exactly being poor but the remarks they make....'

In those days, at least they sought out the indigent old

players. Who knows where the hundreds of old County ex-players, still living, are now? Or who cares?

A lot of them are drawing a thing called Social Security or living on the pension. Ooh, aye.

Sometimes it's pathetic to see great old players trying to find someone to buy them a drink or a feed or give them a cigarette. If they get invited to a cricket dinner they tuck in – it's a luxury.

Of course, things have improved a little as the years have gone by. The Cricketers Friendly Society has done a great job but, of course, it's very short of funds.

So George and Alf started looking every day in the Jobs Vacant columns of the newspapers.

But no luck, until one day they saw an advertisement for two footmen to work on the carriage of His Grace at one of the big houses in the district.

Now, this wasn't exactly what they were looking for: the life they'd been used to didn't exactly fit them for this menial task – but beggars can't be choosers, as the saying goes.

So they applied for the job and got an interview.

And they arrived bang on time, as usual (professional cricketers learn to be punctual at all times).

Outside the big gate, George said to Alf: 'Not exactly what we want, but tha must admit it be better than cutting down willow trees.'

And Alf, a bit nervous, replied: 'Ooh, aye, that's if we get it.'

So up the wide gravel path they go, through the spacious grounds to the grand old mansion.

On the verandah, they took off their caps, and a butler opened the door and they told him they were the applicants.

So the butler told them to wait and eventually they were taken in to see Her Grace the Lady of the House.

Very courteous were the retired cricketers, weren't they? They'd attended a few cocktail parties and met a few toffs when they were still playing cricket.

So they bowed and shook hands with Her Grace.

And she says: 'I'm afraid these jobs as footmen will mean long, arduous hours standing on the back of the coach and opening the doors for me or my guests. You'll be on your feet for many hours – so you will need to have strong legs.'

So George said: 'Well, Your Grace, I've always had strong,

thick legs. In fact, you have to have, to be a fast bowler – and I were a quickee for Yorkshire for near twenty year. And my mate has got strong legs, too. Haven't you, Alf?'

George nudged his nervous mate.

And Alf managed to say: 'Ooh, aye, I were a seam bowler and an outfielder, Your Grace, that I were.'

Her Grace replied: 'How interesting. Well, would you mind rolling up your trousers to let me feel the calves of your legs? One has to be sure when employing servants.'

George gulped and said 'Ooh, aye,' and began to roll up his trouser legs.

Alf followed his mate's example only after receiving a sharp dig in the ribs.

So Her Grace inspected their legs, holding her lorgnette. Then she felt their calves – much to Alf's embarrassment.

And she said: 'Very strong, very strong indeed. I'm quite sure you'll be capable of standing on the coach for long hours. But also you'll be required to act as servants when I entertain, so your strong legs will come in handy, as you'll be wearing puttees around your lovely calves.'

Alf looked at George with a doubtful air.

Nothing loth, Her Grace continued: 'And you'll have to carry heavy silver trays with the drinks which, of course, means you'll need to have strong arms and good biceps.'

So George said: 'No problems, Your Grace, we both worked in the pits and tha develops good biceps down there, as you probably know. And we built up our biceps over twenty year playing cricket for Yorkshire. Didn't we, Alf?'

'Ooh, aye,' Alf said, still very nervous indeed.

Her Grace said: 'That sounds fine but would you mind taking off your coats and letting me inspect your biceps?'

Well, Alf looked sideways at George who nodded his approbation, and they took off their jackets and rolled up their sleeves.

Her Grace felt their biceps with caressing hands and she said: 'How muscular they are – how strong they feel. You'll be able to carry the heavy trays with ease, I feel sure. How strong they feel.'

So they put their coats back on.

And Her Grace said: 'I'm sure you will be very suitable but I'll just have to consult my husband, His Grace. Would you be

'Now would you mind showing me your testimonials?'

so kind as to be seated for a moment?'

She left the room and George and Alf sat on red chairs fringed with gold brocade.

George winked and said: 'Relax. We've got a good chance wi' this job.'

And Alf gulped and said: 'Ooh, aye.'

Her Grace soon returned and she said: 'Well, His Grace agrees. There is just one more thing: would you mind showing me your testimonials?'

Well, on the way out, as they were walking along the gravel path, Alf said: 'You know what I reckon?'

And George said: 'What?'

And Alf said: 'If we hadn't a been so bloody ignorant, we'd have got that job!'

20
A Punishment to Fit the Crime

Fred Trueman

I get all kinds of strange requests on the phone for charities and God knows what; but the strangest I ever got was in 1975, during the Australian tour of England.

The phone rang at home and I answered.

A deep voice said: 'Mr Trueman?'

I said: 'Yes.'

'This is the Social Security here.'

I thought, Fred, you've made it, a big car and a big house, sitting on your backside, and on the dole as well. This is the way to live, I'm in.

I said: 'Yes, what is it?'

He said: 'We'd like you to help us.'

I said: 'Well, I have been helping you since I were fourteen.'

So he said: 'No, we're serious.'

I said: 'Well, so am I, very serious; but what can I do for you?'

And he said: 'You know the Test wicket that's been dug up at Headingley?'

I said: 'Oh, yes, and the people that did it should have been hung.'

He said: 'Well, we agree with you but we can't do those things these days, the law won't allow us. I'm phoning you from the jail; I'm one of the warders. We have those culprits who did it in the cell and they have locked and barricaded themselves in and we can't get them out.'

So I said: 'Well, what can I do?'

And he said: 'Well, it's a funny thing but they say you are the only person they will speak to, and so is there any possible chance of you calling at the jail because if you can get in the cell and get it open we can talk to them and reason.'

I said: 'I'll do my best. I've got to go up to Yorkshire Television tomorrow and I usually pass Armley jail, and make sure I don't stop, don't I? But if that's what you want I'll call tomorrow.'

So the next day I parked my car and I knocked on this iron door, and I heard the bolts and a warder opened this door and said: 'Come in, Fred.'

In I went, the door shut behind me, three bolts and four locks, and I thought, 'Christ, they're going to let me out of

'Freddie Trueman . . . '

here, aren't they?' Then through another little door about three yards away, same procedure, through another one, same procedure, then I came to a passage about four feet wide, and I asked: 'What's this?'

They said: 'That's the exercise yard.'

I said: 'Thank you.' So I took two strides and I was across that. Then I went up these iron steps outside this building, through another iron door, on to this iron platform, and thought this is just like a West Indian cricket ground - all barbed wire and wire netting, fabulous. So, I went along, and I got to cell 23 and I knocked on the door and a voice asked: 'Who's that?' And I said: 'Freddie Trueman.'

'Hang on a minute, Fred,' and they were crashing and banging and eventually the door opened.

I went in and I sat on the wooden form, and there in front of me were these culprits, and I said: 'Now. What have you been doing then?'

They said: 'You know what we've done, Fred, we've dug the Test wicket up, and they've caught us and we're here.'

And I said: 'And so you should be, and you should be hung as well for what you did. You spoiled the pleasure of 160 million people around the world through your vandalism.'

They said: 'We couldn't care less about that, we've got publicity for our cause.'

So I said: 'Fair enough, everybody wants publicity for a cause, and you got it, but it was a nasty way to do it. Anyway, what can I do for you?'

So they said: 'Well, it's like this. We're a bit worried about the sentence we're going to receive.'

I said: 'Well, you haven't been tried yet, so you don't know.'

They said: 'No, but we've heard a nasty rumour.'

I said: 'What's that?'

And they said: 'They reckon we're going to have to jump off the stand at Headingley and Keith Fletcher's going to try to catch us.'

21
Famous Last Words:
'It was your call, wasn't it?'

Fred Trueman

I always admired Len Hutton. He was the greatest batsman who played during my career. He had perfect balance and always seemed to have plenty of time to play his shots.

But we didn't seem to get on personally: perhaps that was because Len didn't seem to have much of a sense of humour. But I must admit he did have a nice turn of sarcasm, as a Southern reporter found out one day at The Oval.

Len Hutton was batting with Denis Compton. It was Len's call and Denis, always an erratic runner, was run out.

This smart Southern reporter waited for Len to come in at the tea interval, and he minced up to Len and said: 'It was your call, wasn't it, Hutton?'

Len looked at him with that bored expression of his and replied: 'When you're running with Denis, you don't call, you pray.'

22

The World's Most Pessimistic Cricketer

Frank Hardy

A pessimist is a person of gloomy and complaining temperament. He always expects the worst – and it usually happens. His prophecies of doom are usually self-fulfilling.

There was this pessimistic County cricketer who said one day when going in to bat: 'It'd be just my luck to get caught in the middle of a hat trick.'

And he was.

Another day, he said: 'I'm so unlucky that if that famous wicket-keeper with the wooden leg caught the ball off his gammy stump instead of my bat I'd be given out.'

And he was.

He had a chequered career as a cricketer. Though he was a very capable batsman, he was always pessimistic. So his team mates nicknamed him Calamity.

He often said: 'I'm too unlucky, I'll never make a century. Something always goes wrong.'

Then, when at last he made it through the 'nervous nineties' and got his first hundred, Calamity started to say he'd never make a double century.

So, one day, he was 197 not out and he said to the wicket-keeper: 'I won't make the double hundred. I'm too unlucky.'

In desperation, he went for a hook shot. It flew high and fast – and looked like a certain six. His team-mates were delighted: a double hundred should overcome his pessimism.

The worst fielder in the opposing side ran around the fence nearly fifty yards and, just as Calamity was in the middle of his third run, took a one-handed catch as the ball was about to go over the fence for six. He was out for 199 – and never ever made a double hundred.

The lads in the dressing-room grabbed the crash helmets

which had been especially issued by the club to be worn when Calamity came back after some bad luck.

On his way back to the pavilion, he threw one of his batting gloves into the members' stand then, in the dressing-room, threw his bat through a window, one of his pads into the toilet, the other over the balcony.

One of his team-mates said: 'Don't get upset. It was a great innings – and that was a brilliant catch.

And Calamity replied: 'I know it was a brilliant catch – but why did it have to happen to me?'

Just then, a well-dressed stranger walked into the dressing room and said to Calamity: 'That was a wonderful innings and I want to reward you.'

And he handed Calamity a cheque for a hundred guineas.

His club mates congratulated Calamity.

He said: 'I didn't like the look of that fellow. Be just my luck for this bloody cheque to bounce.'

And it did.

Calamity continued to make more than his share of runs, in spite of his increasingly despondent attitude. And people began to say that he might be Test material.

But Calamity used to say: 'I'll never get selected for England: I make a noise drinking my soup.'

So, when he was going to a cricket luncheon, one of his friends said: 'Don't order soup.'

After the luncheon, Calamity said: 'What did I tell you? They were all watching me when I was making a noise drinking my soup.'

'I told you not to order soup,' his friend reminded him.

'I didn't. The lunch was self-service,' Calamity explained. 'Anyway, they'd pick anyone before me, even a parson.'

And David Sheppard was selected in the next English team, and Calamity was passed over.

He took to saying: 'I'll never reach double figures again in any innings, as long as I live.'

And he didn't.

So he was dropped from his County team, faded into obscurity and was soon forgotten in cricketing circles.

In his private life, his pessimistic prognostications began to come true even more often and so he became very suspicious, even paranoid.

Never got selected

So late one night, years after he had retired from cricket, he was standing waiting for a bus, when a well-dressed, long-haired youth asked him the time.

And Calamity said: 'You know what will happen if I tell you the time? Well, I'll tell you. We'll get to talking, see, and before we know where we are you'll have missed your last bus.'

Well, this young bloke couldn't believe his ears. 'Look,' he said. 'I just asked you the time. I haven't got a watch...'

Calamity looked at him suspiciously. 'You haven't got a watch? You're well-dressed. You've got a job, haven't you?'

The young fellow wondered what he had struck. 'Yes, I've got a good job. And there's no need for us to get to talking...'

'But we are talking, aren't we?' Calamity said. 'Was that your last bus that just went by? What did I tell you? You've missed your last bus. Now, I'm an hospitable man. I can't let you sleep in the park or walk home. Next thing, I'll invite you home to my place. That's your caper, isn't it?'

By this time, the young bloke was getting worried. 'But I only asked you for the time,' he said.

'That's what you say now,' Calamity persisted pessimistically. 'But I'll invite you home. And you'll meet my wife. She's a kind-hearted woman and she'll make you up a bed in the spare room so you can sleep at our place. And tomorrow morning at breakfast I'll introduce you to my daughter who's a sweet kid of sixteen. And you'll take a fancy to her. I know your type, a lady-killer with pointy shoes and stove-pipe trousers and sideboards. Just the type to turn a young girl's head with your slimy, cunning ways.'

The young fellow tried to get a word in, but Calamity was in full flight: 'Don't argue with me. I know your type, a philanderer from way back. And I'm good-hearted, see, gullible. I wouldn't wake up to you, see. And you'd end up staying for three months and you'll start taking my daughter out. And me and my wife will lay awake at night, worried stiff. And then one day you'll disappear and our poor little daughter will tell us that you've put her in the family way – and walked out on her.'

The young bloke was desperate: 'I'm sorry, but all I did was ask you the time.'

Calamity glared at him with a paranoid air: 'Now, you see where a thing like that can lead. But do you know what I'll do to you when you put my lovely daughter in the family way? I'll find yer, mate, I'll find you if you go to the other end of the earth. And I'll have a gun with me and I'll shoot you stone bloody dead!'

Calamity grabbed the young man by the shiny lapels of his coat. 'And do you know what they'll do to me? They'll find me guilty of murder and put me in jail for the term of my natural life. That's what they'll do to me.'

The young fellow was shaking with fright.

Calamity pushed him against the post of the bus stop, and yelled: 'And I'll end up spending the rest of my life in jail – all because a flash bastard like you was too miserly to buy a watch!'

23
'I've had an accident'

Fred Trueman

I've been a very lucky man to have travelled the whole wide world playing the great game cricket. Think of all the exotic places I've visited – like Belfast and Bombay.

I had one trip to India. Well, anybody who goes to India twice should get a V C as big as a frying pan. I don't care how strong your stomach is, their food'll get through it. I've seen people there playing cricket with me lose two stone in a fortnight, and they weren't on a diet.

In India, if you go for a swim you can be bitten by a water snake and you're dead in nine seconds. After you've been there three weeks you go looking for one, the food is so bad.

It's a well known fact that to come back to England after a five-month tour of India and break wind is a luxury.

In 1936, I think it was, or '35, Lord Tennyson took the England touring team to India, and they played in Bombay, in a Test Match.

India won the toss and batted. England went out to field and the famous bowler called Alf Gover, from Surrey, marked out his run and had a trial run-up.

Then the Indian batsman faced up, took guard, and the umpire said: 'Play.'

And Alf Gover set off on his run-up with the first ball of the match. He came thundering in – straight past the umpire and the batsman at his end and he kept going.

Straight down the wicket, past the startled batsman at the other end, and he kept going – between first slip and the wicket-keeper and he carried on, brushing third man to one side, up the pavilion steps, and he'd gone.

We'd like to get on with the game

After a while, the amateur Captain of England, Lord Tennyson, asked himself a question. Whereabouts is Gover? So he went off the field, into the dressing room, up into the pavilion and said: 'Gover, Gover, where are you?'

And a voice answered: 'I'm in here.'

And he went through and he asked: 'Where's "here"?'

He said: 'I'm in the toilet, sir.'

Lord Tennyson asked: 'What's the matter with you, Gover?'

Gover replied: 'Well, as a matter of fact, sir, I've had an accident.'

And Lord Tennyson said: 'Well, would you give me the ball back, we'd like to get on with the game!'

24
Famous Last Words:
'I've got him in two minds'

Frank Hardy

There was this crafty bowler who always wanted to bowl all day (no name, no pack drill).

Hated the Captain to take him off, always tried to talk him out of it.

'I'm just finding a length, skipper,' he'd say, even when his figures were none for plenty.

One day, he was getting hit into the fence and over it.

The Captain came up to say he was taking him off.

'Give me another over,' the crafty bowler said. 'I've got him in two minds.'

'Yeh,' says the Captain. 'He doesn't know whether to hit you for four or six. I'm taking you off.'

25

The Fluker

Frank Hardy

The greatest fluker who ever picked up a bat, the number one, grade 'A', all-time champion fluker was Fred Fullarton, who played for a certain county years ago.

To fluke means to score by accident in a game of skill. A fluke is something that juts out of an instrument, like the hook on an anchor or the barb of a harpoon. And Fred Fullarton had, in the immortal words of a famous fast bowler, more edges on his bat than a cracked pisspot.

Fullarton became known as Fluker Fred, then simply as the Fluker. And, like most men who have apt nicknames, his real name was soon forgotten.

The Fluker's intended cover drive usually went for four – off the inside edge of his bat, between his pads and the leg stump; his intended on-drive or mid-wicket shot usually went for four – off the outside edge, between third slip and gully. His favourite shot, which he played best, was the drive between first and second slip for four.

A ball outside the off stump, he either edged for four or missed altogether.

In fact, he usually played at and missed the really good deliveries, the ones that would miss his stumps, that is. Somehow he managed to hit the straight ones.

It has been alleged, again by this certain fast bowler, that the Fluker had perfected the play and miss shot. Where other players went to the nets to practise hitting the ball, he practised missing it until he had the knack of playing at a dangerous ball – and missing it – down to a fine art.

The Fluker could make a big score, even a century, without playing for one shot – and without really giving a definite chance. He often hit a ball in the air close to a fieldsman, but rarely put one to hand.

Of course, everyone knew he was a fluker; except the Fluker himself, that is - not the least of his amazing inclinations being his belief that he played for every shot.

But he had the scores on the board, was always well up in the averages, so the committee were well satisfied (they were usually a hundred miles away and didn't see many of his performances) and he kept his place in the side.

In later years, the Fluker always said that his greatest performance was the day he saved the match against Yorkshire.

In the second innings, his team needed 300 to win - and had lost four wickets for less than thirty runs - and two of the men out were England batsmen.

The situation looked hopeless when the Fluker came in to take a hand in the proceedings. The ball was swinging and seaming, and the pitch was taking spin. No way the match could be saved except by a flood and there wasn't a cloud in the sky.

But the old Fluker was undeterred. He told the lads in the dressing-room: 'I'm the only batsman in the world who can get a big score under these conditions and save this game.'

And his team mates didn't deny it: in a strange way what he had said was true.

So the Fluker walked to the wicket, with his comical ten past ten walk, looking his immaculate self: flannels and shirt clean and freshly pressed; pads as white as snow (he carried whitening fluid in his kitbag); his boots were also shining white and he'd painted the soles and heels black to achieve contrast.

His bat was freshly waxed - and sand-papered down to take some of the dents off its edges.

'Good Lord,' one of the bowlers said, 'here comes the play and miss expert.'

At the crease the Fluker looked around to see where the fielders were, then took guard.

'Two legs, please, Mister umpire.'

He took two different guards which he marked with a piece of chalk he carried in his hip pocket (none of your mark it with the toe of your boot for the Fluker).

Then he inspected the field again to check that none of the tykes had moved while his back was turned, for all the world as if he could place the ball between fieldsmen any time he wanted to. Then he made sure his gloves were tight, his protector and thigh pad in position.

He got off the mark with a drive between first and second slip for four, then played at and missed a couple, then took a single for a shot between his legs to square leg off the last ball of the over.

He was playing for the strike, the old Fluker, wasn't he?

Now, the bowler who now came on was one of the few left in County cricket who still believed that the Fluker was easy to get out. In fact, he was the self-same cheeky fast bowler who used the indelicate term 'cracked pisspot' to describe the Fluker's precious bat.

'I know how to get him out, Captain,' he said, as he took the ball.

'Do you?' the Captain said.

And the fast bowler said: 'Ooh, aye, I'll bowl him a straight one.'

And he did – but the Fluker sent it flying – off an inside edge to the fine leg boundary.

He scored off every ball, for once not using his play and miss shot, and took twelve runs from the over.

After bowling three more expensive overs, during which he once knelt down and banged his head on the ground in sheer frustration as the Fluker edged him all over the ground, the fast bowler was taken off.

The Captain tried four other bowlers without success and the Fluker reached fifty with a mid-wicket shot down the gully – and doffed his cap to the largely ironic cheers from the crowd.

The famous fast bowler said to the Fluker: 'Where are you playing in your next match?'

The Fluker said: 'Belfast.'

And the bowler replied: 'Well, don't bother buying an air ticket: with your luck you'll be able to walk it.'

But the Fluker ignored the sarcasm and moved steadily towards his century. Meanwhile, wickets had fallen and the Fluker advised each incoming batsman: 'Let me have the bowling, I can save this match.'

From time to time, the Fluker had the sight screen moved and got on everyone's nerves, especially those of the bowlers, by having long sessions giving advice to his batting partner.

At 75, he hit a ball straight to a fieldsman on the full for the first time and was caught – but the umpire had called: 'No ball!'

As he approached the hundred mark, the old Fluker used his play and miss shot to great advantage: but always the ball just went over or past the stumps.

He reached his century with a six. Now, there was only one way he could score a six: go for the hook off a quick bowler and make contact with the back edge of his bat. This he somehow managed to do and the ball went over the fence at fine leg.

The cheers were louder and more ironic than before, and the Fluker acknowledged them by touching his cap and waving his bat.

Another wicket fell, but the total had passed the two hundred mark and the Yorkshire lads were getting worried.

The Captain had tried every usable bowler without success, and no one wanted to have another go. He stood there scratching his head.

The Fluker said to the new batsman: 'Get a single if you can, and give me the strike.'

'Sure,' the batsman said. 'You can have it.' He knew that he couldn't make runs under the conditions, not having the Fluker's kind of luck.

The Fluker then advised him how to play each bowler and concluded: 'I'll be taking things steady for a while, I'm going for my first double century.'

'And you're sure to get it,' his new partner said with an unnoticed edge of sarcasm, 'the way you're playing.'

The Captain came to a decision and threw the ball to the famous fast bowler: 'Have another go at him. He might try something now that he's got his ton.'

'You've got to be jokin',' the fast bowler said. 'I'll go bald and grey before my time bowling at this fella. He plays across the line with a cross bat, yet he never gives a chance.'

But the Captain insisted, so the fast bowler hurled down a bumper and the Fluker back-edged it for two down to deep fine leg.

The fast men bowled three overs each at him but he went his merry way, playing and missing, edging and fluking until he had approached 150 - and his team needed less than 70 runs to win.

Yorkshire could see certain victory slipping through their fingers.

The cheeky fast bowler said to the Captain: 'I've got no air left. I've pulled everything out. I'm down to skin, my head's bleeding from frustration. But I've got one card left. A slower one, pitched on the leg stump and swinging away to take the off stump. And, if he edges it for four - I'll hang for him!'

It was one of the best outswingers ever bowled - and it seemed to take the leg stump. No one doubted that the ball hit the wicket or that the legside bail went up. The fielding side cheered for the sheer relief of seeing the last of their tormentor - and the fast bowler shouted lurid curses of joy.

But then the strangest twist ever to occur in cricket was witnessed: the bail fell back into position again.

Both umpires inspected the wicket and it was intact. The bowler and fieldsmen gathered around to observe the Eighth Wonder of the World.

The umpires at last announced that the ball must have squeezed between the leg and middle stumps and, because they were driven tight into hard summer ground, the bail must have fallen back into position between them.

The verdict was: 'Not out!'

The Fluker didn't turn a hair.

He got an enormous cheer for his 150, an on-drive between third slip and gully, just passing the outstretched hand of each fielder. The Fluker had made the shot so often that not only he, but sections of the crowd, thought he had played for it.

Someone in the crowd yelled: 'Bowl him up an axe and see if he can edge that.'

The fast bowler said: 'Please, Captain, I beg you, take me off, before I kill him'

The Captain said: 'He's knocked every other bowler out of the game. It's you - or one of the spectators.'

So the fast bowler kept at it and the Fluker kept edging.

The fast bowler said: 'Your bat has more edges than an old threepenny bit.'

The Fluker replied: 'I shall tell you something. I paid for this bat with my own money, so I shall use all of it.'

The fast bowler said: 'The only part of it you haven't used is the middle.'

The more frustrated and angry the bowlers became, the more the Fluker calmly fluked.

The cheeky fast bowler asked: 'Have you ever thought of joining the church? You should. With your luck, you'd soon be Archbishop of Canterbury.'

The wicket-keeper asked the Fluker: 'Have you got any children?'

'Yes, one.'

'That must have been a bloody fluke, too.'

But nothing could ruffle the Fluker and soon he had 196 against his name and his team needed only five runs to win – with five minutes to go and nine wickets down.

The fast man was still bowling and he sent down another outswinger, pitched leg, swinging away late to the off. Would have bowled Bradman or Hutton neck and crop.

The Fluker went for a big drive – and edged the ball into the slips at a comfortable catching height. But, by some miracle known only to the god who protects flukers, the ball was just out of the reach of both first and second slip and sailed to the boundary.

The Fluker had made his first and only double hundred, and he had saved the match – and he looked insufferably smug as he doffed his cap and waved his bat.

On the balcony of the pavilion, his team-mates clapped half-heartedly. They had been embarrassed by the whole performance. But, after all, the Fluker had turned the match. Trouble was, what could they say to him when he returned to the pavilion?

Then, with the scores level, off the very next ball he went for his cover drive just once again and, to the amazement of one and all, middled it. He hit it with the middle of the bat! And it went like a rocket through the covers about six inches above the ground.

The man at cover recovered from the shock in time to put his hand down and the ball stuck in it.

The Fluker was out at last for 200 – and he was heard to mutter to the not-out batsman as he walked away: 'How unlucky can you be? I gave my first chance and got out to a miracle catch.'

He doffed his cap as he came to the gate – and looked up to the balcony. But no one was there.

His team-mates had fled: they were too embarrassed to face him.

So the old Fluker had a bath and changed. As he was leaving the ground he saw one of his team-mates. 'Where were you and the lads when I came in?' he asked.

'Oh, I rushed out to ring my wife and tell her what a great innings she missed,' his colleague replied. 'And the other lads, well, er, they were so moved they couldn't have faced you without bursting into tears. They'll talk about that innings for the rest of their lives.'

The Fluker went home well pleased with himself.

A week later the firm he worked for promoted him and made him a director. They reasoned he was a famous sportsman, with an excellent temperament.

Eventually, like all cricketers, the Fluker retired – but he didn't end up on the scrap heap. He made a nice living lecturing on the art of batting, coaching at schools and commenting on cricket for a regional radio station.

He often spoke of the time he made a double hundred against Yorkshire and saved the match. 'It was a bowler's paradise,' he would point out, 'and I can say with due modesty I was the only batsman who could have done it.'

In the living-room of his comfortable house, the Fluker has, to this day, several cricket trophies. His favourite is a diagram of the shots he played the day he made his double century. The club scorer drew the diagram for him and it hangs in a handsome frame above the fireplace.

Of course, the diagram doesn't show how he played the shots, only where the ball went.

Visitors often admire the diagram.

Of course, occasionally an old cricketer will get technical and say: 'Nearly all the shots were behind the wicket. You must have had a lot of luck that day.'

And the Fluker will reply: 'You need a bit of luck to make a double hundred. Even Bradman and Hutton needed a bit of luck. Anyway, I always was a better player behind the wicket than in front of it.'

26
The Influence of Soup on Cricket

Frank Hardy

There must have been a lot of tragic – and funny – stories about men who almost played for England or Australia but didn't quite make it, or who almost toured for their country and didn't quite make it.

They had the ability but somehow the selectors passed them over – and not always for reasons directly related to cricket.

In at least two cases, the attitude of a cricketer to soup caused him to be 'missing' when the Test team was listed.

How is that possible?

Well, take the case of Les Jackson, a top-class fast bowler who did make it into the English side, but only twice.

A certain fellow cricketer (another fast bowler in fact) recalls that, on one occasion, at the height of his career, Les was at a cricket dinner on some big occasion.

The waiters served that refined French cold soup.

Les called out to his fast-bowling mate: 'Hey, Fred! They've forgot to warm up the soup.'

The Amateurs and Gentlemen present were not amused and made a note of the transgression.

Anyway, Les Jackson never again played for England, though plenty of good judges thought he should have.

Of course, I can't vouch for the actual gospel truth of Les Jackson's case, but I can when it comes to the reason why Bert Ironmonger, the Victorian bowler, never ever got a trip to England.

Bert Ironmonger was, by profession, a garbage-carter in one of the less affluent suburbs of Melbourne, and not noted for his table manners.

Nor for his batting. He always used to go in number eleven and never reached double figures in his long career. (On one occasion, his wife rang him at the Melbourne Cricket Ground. A voice answered the telephone and said: 'He's just gone in to bat, Mrs Ironmonger. Hold the line: he won't be a minute.')

Bert Ironmonger was perhaps the greatest orthodox leg-break bowler who played in living memory. He would have been suited to English conditions – but the selectors passed him by every time the team was announced to visit the Old Country.

Well, the old Bert eventually retired from cricket and, after twenty years, just about everyone had forgotten him – when he turned up as a star guest on a radio programme called Fifty and Over.

The format of the programme was an interview with some person over fifty who had, at one time, been in the public eye.

'He's just gone in to bat – he won't be a minute...'

Well, the interviewer asked Bert Ironmonger a lot of questions about his career as a cricketer, needless to say, and Bert did his best.

Until, at last, he asked Bert: 'You never ever got a trip to England with an Australian touring team. In view of your outstanding record, how do you explain that?'

'Oh, I used to make a noise drinking my soup,' Bert Ironmonger replied, without as much as a grin on his face.

Which just goes to show that a lot of things can influence Test selectors – including soup.

27

The Funniest Match I Ever Played In

Fred Trueman

Every old cricketer, looking back over his career, can remember something about nearly every match he played in. Usually, he remembers best the funny incidents.

Well, the funniest cricket match I ever played in – and I played in quite a few – was the Combined Services against Australia at Kingston-on-Thames in 1953.

I was just at the end of my two years of service in the RAF. And, you might find this hard to believe, but they were amongst the happiest of my life: the comradeship, the other side of life, the discipline. I came out with a sense of self-respect and discipline that stood me in good stead in later years.

Well, my last job for the RAF came when I was chosen, or rather invited, to play for the Combined Services team against Australia, the proceeds of the game to go to the RAF Benevolent Fund. That was the year England won back the Ashes from Australia after a gap of something like twenty-six years.

So I turned up at Kingston. Australia won the toss and batted. They opened with an old pal of mine, Arthur Morris, a very fine left-hand batsman. In that Australian team were some formidable names: Lindwall, Miller, Harvey, de Courcey, Benaud, to mention a few who have gone down in history.

Of course, I was cock-a-hoop, walking on air: I had been a member of the England side that had just regained the Ashes.

And I expected to bowl the first over, so I immediately marked out my run up.

Now, the Combined Services' Captain that day was not the usual Captain I had played under in earlier services matches, a man named Alan Shirreff, whom I admired and respected.

Oh, no, the Captain that day was a Commander from the Navy and I had met him once previously, hadn't I? And I didn't take a great liking to him, shall I say.

Well, he came over to me and he said: 'What are you doing, Trueman?'

And I said: 'I'm marking out my run-up because I usually bowl the first over.'

'Oh, do you?' he replied.

And I said: 'Yes, usually.'

And he said: 'Well, not today.'

So a young fellow from the Army was given the new ball, and he knew me and he said: 'Don't worry, Fred, I'll bowl into the wind.'

Next thing, I went to leg slip, where I always fielded, even for England.

The Captain said: 'And what do you think you are doing, now, Trueman?'

I said: 'Well, I usually field at leg slip.'

Then Alan Shirreff, who was playing although not Captain, came over and said on my behalf: 'Well, he does field there usually. In fact, he's considered one of the four best leg-slip fielders and catches in the world. And, in case you didn't notice, he played for England last week and this is where he fielded and took catches.'

The Captain replied: 'Not in my team. The Major has fielded in this position for years. You can go to fine leg, Trueman.'

So I went to fine leg.

Well, we got a couple of quick wickets. I didn't get any, but the Army bloke did.

Then the great Keith Miller came in and he edged the first ball bowled to him, straight to the Major at leg slip.

The Major never laid a finger on it.

Keith Miller was off the mark – and he made us pay for the Major's missed catch: he got a double century and so did Jim de Courcey.

At one stage towards the end of the day, our Captain put

the Major on to bowl. I'd seen better bowlers in the Dales League.

Australia made God knows how many: at least five hundred – and I finished up with nout for 96.

And they defeated us by an innings: Lindwall and Miller saw to that.

Well, after the match, in the dressing-room, the Captain came over to me and he said: 'Trueman, I'd like a word with you.'

I said: 'What is it?'

And he said: 'I'll tell you, here and now, you will never play for the Combined Services again.'

And I said: 'Those are the only true words you have spoken all day. You're right. I was demobbed yesterday.'

For, unbeknown to the Captain, I had been demobilized from the R A F the day before the match finished – and had only stayed on to do my stint for the Benevolent Fund.

The Captain, the Navy Commander, had been a County cricketer. And I looked forward to the day when I could play against him in County cricket. But the chance never came.

Perhaps it's just as well, because I would have played a concerto on his ribs fit for Tchaikovsky.

28
Famous Last Words: 'There'll be no more run-outs'

Fred Trueman

Sam Cook and Tom Goddard, the great Gloucester spin-bowling combination, were each useful batsmen, even though they came in at number ten and eleven.

Trouble was, they were often bad callers and very erratic runners between the wickets, so that if Sam didn't run Tom out, the chances were that Tom would run Sam out.

George Emmett, then Captain, got sick of them running each other out.

So George Emmett said: 'Now, listen, you lads, there'll be no more run-outs. If either of you runs the other out in the next match, I'm going to suspend you both for two matches without pay.'

Well, as it turned out, Sam and Tom were both injured – but they insisted on batting in the second innings, each with a runner.

Well, we had to laugh, didn't we?

There they were, the two worst callers in the game batting with runners.

So Sam hit one and there's an easy single in it, so he called and off goes his runner.

Tom's runner headed down the pitch, too, but Tom yelled: 'Go back,' to Sam's runner.

Sam's runner went back, so he and Tom's runner ended up beside Sam Cook at the crease.

Tom Goddard remembered his Captain's warning and got excited, did Tom. So he ran himself, limping down until all four, the two batsmen and the two runners, were at the same end.

Well, there was a run-out, needless to say, and the innings is finished.

Sam Cook and Tom Goddard came off the field (followed by their runners) waving their bats to the ribald shouts of the crowd.

Their Captain, George Emmett, laughed so much, he forgot to suspend them.

29

Famous Last Words: 'You can't give me out leg before from there'

Frank Hardy

Years ago, in a bush match in Australia, a visiting player came in to bat and was amazed to find the only umpire standing behind cover-point.

As he walked by, he said to the umpire: 'What are you doing there? You should be at the bowler's end.'

'It's none of your business where I stand,' the umpire replied.

'Yes, it is. You can't give a leg before decision from there,' the batsman persisted.

'Never mind trying to tell me how to do my job,' the umpire snapped. 'You get in there and bat.'

No sooner had the batsman taken guard when the first ball rapped him on the pads. There was a loud appeal and the umpire gave him out leg before – from behind cover-point.

As the batsman walked back to the pavilion, the umpire said: 'What'd I tell you, yer mug? Thought you said I couldn't give you out leg before from here?'

From behind cover point . . .

30

How Sam Loxton was Trapped at Square Leg

Frank Hardy

Someday, someone ought to make a list of things ruined by war - including the careers of a lot of good cricketers.

Take Ken Meuleman, the talented Victoria opening batsman. He was just about to break into the Australian team when the Second World War broke out. Then came five years with no cricket to speak of, no international cricket, anyway. Meuleman played again after the war ended in 1945 - but was selected for Australia only once, and that against New Zealand.

Then take an even sadder example: coincidentally another Ken, the late Ken Farnes. He was six feet four inches tall. He actually played in a Test Match against Australia at the Oval in 1938. He is famous for the fact that he clean bowled Gimblett, Hammond and Hardstaff in quick succession. Farnes was killed in a flying accident in Scotland when serving in the RAF.

But then, you could say that Bradman and Hutton had five lost years during the Second World War. The mind boggles at the thought of the record books if that war hadn't slightly interrupted those two careers.

Then, of course, there was Sam Loxton, the Australian all-rounder: hard-hitting batsman and medium-paced bowler.

But the difference with Sam was that he made bloody sure the war didn't interrupt his cricketing career. He kept in peak form throughout - by practising every day and organizing a cricket match at the drop of a hat, wherever he happened to be. So he bounced back after the war as good as ever and toured the world playing for Australia.

Sam was an attacking batsman (not like the powder-puff

batsmen these days), always looking for runs. He had one fatal weakness, and that was his tendency to overdo the hook shot.

And that's how this incident was possible: the story of how he was trapped at square leg.

It happened in 1943 at a place called Benson's Valley, a sleepy village about thirty-five miles from Melbourne. Sam Loxton was stationed in an Army camp at a place called Darley, near Benson's Valley.

I lived in Benson's Valley at the time – and was in the Royal Hotel at the very moment that the old Sam walked into the bar. He bought a small beer and sounded out the locals about the chances of organizing a cricket match.

'Just a friendly game,' Sam said, without giving his name, 'between the Darley Army Camp and a Benson's Valley team.'

'All the cricketers are in the Army,' I told Sam, 'like me and you.'

'Couldn't you scratch a side together for a one-day game next Saturday?'

'I doubt it,' I said. 'I can't see the local has-beens wanting to chase leather all day against Sam Loxton, in the middle of the summer.' Noting his surprise at my picking his dial (he had one of those leathery faces like a cricket ball after two hundred runs and weeks in the practice nets), I added: 'Picked you as soon as you walked in the door. You would have been playing for Australia today – if this war hadn't started.'

'I'll play for Australia after the war,' Sam replied. 'If I can keep in practice until it ends.'

'It might never bloody end, mate, the way it's going,' I told him – then went to look for the president of the defunct Benson's Valley Cricket Association.

Well, I found the president, and a match was organized for the following Saturday, eleven o'clock until six.

Benson's Valley fielded a rag-bag team of old cricketers and a couple of soldiers on leave. Sam Loxton brought a well-tutored team of soldiers who had little else to do except play cricket and, as Sam was a Major, they found it difficult to ignore his frequent requests for a 'friendly game'.

Benson's Valley won the toss and batted. They made about

eighty, Sam taking six wickets for very little.

So immediately after lunch the Army team came in to bat, with Sam Loxton himself taking the first ball. He wanted plenty of practice so he began quietly, playing for the strike.

I was not there that day (my leave was up and I had returned to my unit in Darwin), but a mate of mine was umpiring and he swears by the truth of the story of how Sam Loxton was trapped at square leg.

His name was Artful Arty Aitchison and he was, beyond all doubt, the greatest cricket umpire Australia ever produced.

Artful Arty knew the cricket rule-book off by heart. When he sat for the umpiring examination before the committee of the Victoria Cricket Association, Jack Ryder and the other experts tried to trick him with smart questions about obscure rules but they weren't in the hunt. Arty got a 100 per cent pass, the only man to do so in the history of Victoria cricket.

Artful Arty would have become a Test umpire only he was too fond of the gargle (would drink a pint of beer through a cricketer's sock at the end of a five-day match, they reckoned). The gargle has ruined many a good man. His father, Artful Arty Aitchison, Senior, was a good umpire too, but fond of the gargle just like his son.

And they were umpiring on this particular day at Benson's Valley - and the temperature rose to more than a hundred degrees.

Anyway, by three o'clock, the army team was well in front of the local side's score - but Sam Loxton wanted more practice.

By four o'clock, Sam Loxton had reached his century - and the umpires, not to mention the players, were getting very thirsty.

So Artful Arty Aitchison, Junior, approached Sam Loxton and said through dry lips: 'Why don't you retire or declare the innings closed? The pub across the road shuts at six o'clock.'

'I need all the practice I can get,' Sam Loxton told him, 'and the game doesn't finish until six o'clock.'

So Sam batted on until after five o'clock. A couple of tail-enders had fallen - but Sam was on his merry way, playing for the strike and hitting the locals all around the oval.

Artful Arty, Junior, consulted his fellow umpire (his thirsty father), then whispered to the bowler, before taking up

'How's that?'

his umpiring position at square leg.

The bowler acting, it is alleged to this day, on the advice of the square-leg umpire (who had exceeded his official duties), dropped one short outside the leg stump.

Sam Loxton couldn't ever resist the hook shot – and he went for it now.

The ball shot like a rocket straight at Artful Arty, Junior, at square leg. He was standing there thinking, it would be a terrible tragedy if the pub was shut before they got him out.

He had four cricket caps on his head, three white jumpers tied around his neck by their sleeves, a couple of watches on each wrist. The ball was coming straight at his face. He put his hands up and caught it.

'How's that?' the bowler appealed to Artful Arty, Senior, who was umpiring at the bowler's end.

The father hesitated, licked his lips then raised his finger. 'Out!' he said. And he lifted the bails and headed straight for the pub.

Sam Loxton said: 'Hey! You can't give me out caught by the square-leg umpire!'

'Yes, he can,' Arty Aitchison, Junior, said. 'He gave you out because he's thirsty and so am I – and because you've got to be taught the lesson that your fondness for the hook shot will get you trapped at square leg and ruin your promising career.'

With those few well-chosen words, he shook the caps, jumpers and watches into a heap on the grass and followed his father towards the pub.

The two teams went, as well, leaving Sam Loxton standing in the middle of the pitch.

A few more friendly games were played between the Army camp and Benson's Valley – but Sam Loxton always brought his own umpires, after that.

31

'We'll just have to get out of it'

Fred Trueman

One of the greatest blokes I met in cricket was Wilf Wooller. He was an international Rugby Union player for Wales and captained Glamorgan at cricket.

He got blamed for a lot of things he didn't do, did Wilf, but he was a real stalwart of Welsh cricket. On the field he would do anything except murder you but, off the field, he would give you anything. And no matter how grim the situation looked for his team, he battled on.

One day at Bristol, Wilf captained Glamorgan against Gloucester. And Gloucester's Captain was George Emmett. With those two characters on the job, anything might happen – and it did.

Gloucester won the toss and batted. The day was fine and hot, the wicket good.

Wilf Wooller said to his lads: 'Well, we've lost the toss, just our luck: the wicket's going to be a batsman's paradise. But we'll just have to put our heads down and get them out.'

At the end of the day, Gloucester were 443 for four.

Wilf said in the dressing-room: 'We're in trouble, lads, but we'll just have to get out of it.'

So they had a bath and went up to the bar for a pint of beer, just like we always did in those days.

Shall I tell you something? I went into the Yorkshire dressing-room last year and, when I saw the drink tray brought in at twenty-five past six, I had to leave. On the tray were six pints of orange juice, three glasses of milk, half of shandy, a whisky – and a gin and tonic for the fast bowler.

Times have changed in County cricket, Fred, I told myself. And they have changed. Look at Warwickshire: they only want a green one and they'd have a snooker set; and, at Northants and Surrey, they don't issue a County cap, they issue a turban with a peak on it.

Anyway, Wilf Wooller and George Emmett were on their second pint, when George says: 'It's a funny game, cricket, look out there.'

And Wilf Wooller looked out and it weren't raining, it were coming down like stair rods. A terrible night from a beautiful day. And the wicket was uncovered, except for the bowling crease at each end. All the rest was open to the teeming rain.

But Wilf said philosophically: 'Aye. But if we're in trouble tomorrow we'll just have to get out of it, that's all.'

So they drank a few more pints and went to bed at about two o'clock in the morning. Sam Cook and Tom Goddard had been lulled to sleep earlier by the sound of raindrops.

Next day, the violent weather had passed, the sun was hot, the wicket steaming.

And George Emmett declared the Gloucester innings closed and Glamorgan had to bat on the sticky dog of a wicket. So the covers were rolled off the bowling creases and the Glamorgan opening batsmen reluctantly padded up.

Now, in that Gloucester side, were two great England spin bowlers, Sam Cook and Tom Goddard. And they were itching to get at the Glamorgan team on the sticky dog. Sam and Tom couldn't wait: their team mates had to hold them back at the dressing-room door. They would share the ten wickets between them: no chance of the faster bowlers getting an over on this wicket.

For the first time in their lives, they ran through the gate onto the field.

And Wilf Wooller said to his team: 'Now, don't worry, lads, we're in trouble but we'll just have to get out of it.'

So Glamorgan batted – and were all out for 42, which left them the bare 401 behind on the first innings.

Sam Cook had taken six for 20 and Tom Goddard took the other four wickets.

And Wilf Wooller had another chat to his team: 'Now, settle down, lads, I know conditions are bad. We're a circus and we're in trouble – but we'll just have to get out of it.'

So Glamorgan have to go in again, haven't they? And,

before long, they are six for 26. And Sam Cook had taken another four wickets.

And in walked the great Wilf Wooller and the old Wilf had lost his philosophical frame of mind, for once in his life, and was ready for anything except murder. He had to pass Sam Cook on the way – and he couldn't stand the self-satisfied smirk on Sam's face.

So he snarled out of the side of his mouth: 'I'll bet you'd like to bowl at this bloody circus of mine on a wicket like this every day of your life, wouldn't you, Sam?'

But Sam Cook remained diplomatically silent: he made no reply, not a word.

When Wilf Wooller got up to the other end, he banged his bat on the floor hard enough to strike oil and he said to the umpire: 'It's only a formality on this bloody wicket but give me two legs.'

The umpire said: 'You've got them.'

And Wilf said: 'I'm ready for anything.'

In came Sam Cook and he tossed the ball up so you could hear it spinning in the heavy atmosphere.

Wilf Wooller pushed forward, seemed to have it well covered but it struck a very sticky patch, stood up, hit the splice – and went straight into the safe hands of Arthur Milton at short leg.

26 for seven.

Wilf Wooller set off back to the pavilion, and as he passed by, Sam Cook said, out of the side of his mouth: 'Cheerio, ringmaster.'

Tap, tap

32
Famous Last Words:
'I'm entitled to tap the wicket'

Fred Trueman

Some cricket grounds in Yorkshire are built above coal-mine tunnels, aren't they?

Well, that's only natural. But it can lead to problems.

One day in a Yorkshire local competition, the wicket was crumbling a bit and one of the visiting batsmen kept going down and tapping the pitch.

After nearly every ball, he'd go down and tap, tap on the spot with the bottom of his bat.

At last, the umpire said to him: 'You'll have to stop tapping that wicket.'

The batsman said: 'Why? I'm entitled to tap the wicket.'

The umpire said: 'Well, just tap it once more.'

The batsman tapped and the umpire said: 'Listen.'

And they listened and – shall I tell you something? They could hear from deep in the bowels of the earth a distant sound: tap, tap, tap.

The umpire told the batsman: 'That's the lads on the weekend shift tapping back. So, it's like I said: You'll have to stop tapping that wicket. Any more, and they might think there's been an accident.'

33

Famous Last Words: 'Well played!'

Fred Trueman

The humour of understated irony is rare; and a wicket-keeper making more than fifty runs in a Test Match is, well, rare enough.

Yet a wicket-keeper who compiled fifty-three runs in one of the few Test innings he ever played made a remark that was a rare gem of understated irony. And his name is all but forgotten.

He was Arthur Wood. He was a fine 'keeper but was just unlucky to be playing in the same era as the great George Duckworth.

Well, George Duckworth was ill on one of the great occasions of cricket – and Arthur Wood took his place as wicket-keeper for England. He travelled from his home in the North to the South by taxi. When the taxi driver charged him a fiver, he said, 'I only borrowed this car, I didn't want to buy it.'

And that was the day that Len Hutton made 364, to break Don Bradman's world record score for a Test innings.

Practically every batsman made a century. And Arthur Wood contributed a well-made but scarcely noticed fifty-three, going to the wicket with England at 770 for six.

When he came off the field, a Member said to Arthur Wood in the dressing-room: 'Well played, Arthur!'

And Arthur Wood replied: 'Think nothing of it, I always was a good man in a crisis!'

34
The World's Unluckiest Cricketer

Frank Hardy

The World's Unluckiest Cricketer was often in trouble as a teenager.

When his parents bought him his first suit, it was a bargain with two pairs of trousers. First time he wore it, he burned a hole in the coat.

After getting caught stealing cars (the first one he pinched was a police car) he took up kidnapping. He kidnapped an orphan and his parents had to put it through university.

To keep him off the streets, his father encouraged him to take up cricket.

Well, he did and he turned out to have a lot of ability – and his parents were relieved that he had found an outlet.

When he was given his County cap it was three sizes too small. He bought two pairs of creams and a blazer – and burned a hole in the blazer.

As a batsman he rarely played and missed.

He often said: 'You watch me: the first time I play and miss I get out. Other batsmen can play and miss all day and not get out.'

One day he was fielding at short leg. The batsman swept a ball off the middle of the bat and it hit him between the eyes and bounced to first slip, who caught it.

When he came to, the Unluckiest Cricketer tried to claim half the catch in the 100 Guinea Award for the most catches of the season. Naturally, he was told that the slip fielder would be awarded the catch. At the end of the season, that same fielder beat him for the award by one catch.

'What did I tell you? he said. 'I'm the world's unluckiest cricketer.

He got caught in the middle of a hat trick on three occasions.

Once, when he was run out, the decision was so bad that supporters of the opposing team started a riot.

Once, his team compiled a record County score. Every other established batsman made a century – and he got run out for a duck on a doubtful decision.

During one tour with his County, he came back to the hotel late at night to find the scorer in his bed. When he complained to the team Captain, the hotel management made up a bed for him on the top of the bath. The scorer woke the Unluckiest Cricketer at six in the morning and said he would like to have a shower.

Then he got married. They were happy until he started to worry that his wife would be unfaithful. 'Just my luck to marry a beautiful woman and someone take her away.' Then when no one took any interest in his wife he began to worry that she must be a dull woman.

Then they had a lovely baby girl who became the apple of his eye – then he began to worry about when his daughter grew up, some cunning philanderer would put her in the family way and leave her in the lurch.

He invented many sayings to sum up his ill-luck. 'If bad luck was music, I'd be a brass band.' 'If it was raining mansions I'd get hit on the head by a Yorkshire loo.' 'If I fell in a vat full of breasts I'd come up sucking my thumb.'

Once, he nearly made a century at Lords. He was 99 not out and straight drove a ball from a left-arm bowler with tremendous power and set off to run. The bowler, with a brilliant piece of fielding, intercepted the ball and threw it back at the stumps.

The Unluckiest Cricketer turned and threw himself full length, covered from head to toe with dirt – but too late. He was run out by a good yard.

The wicket-keeper, who should have known better, said: 'You're unlucky, all right. That throw was pitched leg and middle and hit the off stump. They even throw leg breaks when they run you out.'

He got to 99 on another occasion and decided to break his luck by hitting his century with a six. He let go a hook behind square leg. The fine leg fielder, who was put there because he had to be put somewhere, had never taken a catch in his life, covered thirty yards and put up his hand.

The ball stuck in it.

The Unluckiest Cricketer said as he walked away: 'What did I tell you? That mug couldn't catch a cold in an epidemic - but he caught me!'

He became very superstitious about his luck. If his stars were bad, he would go back to bed and refuse to play.

It went from bad to worse - until the club committee thought the best thing to do was give him a benefit match as a hint that he should retire.

It rained for three days and nights - and his benefit game was washed out.

Unlike other cricketers, he did nothing to raise money for his own benefit. He didn't even run any raffles.

So two of his team mates got their heads together - and decided to run a big raffle.

One of them was called Good Turn Jackson, who always said: 'If you can't do a man a good turn, never do him a bad one.'

So the old Good Turn announced: 'We'll run a raffle with a first prize of ten thousand pounds: a hundred tickets at a hundred quid each.'

The other fellow asked: 'What good will that do? If the first prize is ten thousand pounds, that leaves nothing for the club's kitty, and provides no benefit for the Unluckiest Cricketer.'

'Just trust me,' said Good Turn.

Good Turn was in all his glory, do-gooding, sticking his nose into other people's business. 'The first prize will be ten thousand quid and the Unluckiest Cricketer will get the lot.'

'How is that possible?'

'I'll tell you how,' Good Turn said. 'I've got a special raffle book printed.' He pulled the book out of his hip pocket. 'A hundred tickets - all number seven.'

Good Turn Jackson waxed enthusiastic: 'We'll raffle ten thousand pounds. The Unluckiest Cricketer will buy a ticket - number seven, needless to say, because all the tickets are number seven - and he'll draw the raffle himself. And, of course, he'll draw his own number and win it. Ten thousand lovely quid. That will cure his inferiority complex. That's what's wrong with him - an inferiority complex. He'll be rich and cured of his complex.'

'There's only three weaknesses in your scheme,' Good Turn's mate said.

'And what are they?'

'Well, firstly, he won't buy a ticket; secondly, where are you going to get ninety-nine mugs to buy a ticket in a rigged raffle for a hundred quid; thirdly, the Unluckiest Cricketer will be in bed because his stars are bad - so he won't draw the raffle.'

Good Turn didn't turn a hair: 'One, he won't have to buy a ticket; I've already bought it. Two, ninety-nine club supporters have already bought tickets for a hundred pounds each. They know the raffle is to put some benefit into the Unluckiest Cricketer's benefit, and they have all agreed not to claim on their tickets. And three, he'll draw the raffle for sure - because that way he'll reckon he can't win it. You have to use psychology.'

So Good Turn went to the house of the Unluckiest Cricketer and found him in bed.

When told about the raffle, he said: 'Not me, I won't buy a ticket in a raffle even for my own benefit. I went into kidnapping once and kidnapped an orphan.'

'No need to buy a ticket,' Good Turn said. 'I've already bought you one. Look, number seven, your lucky number.'

'You mean it used to be my lucky number,' the Unluckiest Cricketer replied. 'That was years ago. Now, I'm the only man in the world without a lucky number.'

'Look,' said Good Turn. 'I've bought you a ticket, the least you can do is take it.'

'I don't want to hurt your feelings but I'm the world's unluckiest cricketer. I'm so unlucky that one time I went on a blind date and she turned out to be an old aunt of mine.'

'Tell you what, you can draw the raffle yourself,' Good Turn persisted. 'That way you can't win it.' The old Good Turn was the best amateur shrink in the country. That hooked the Unluckiest Cricketer.

He got out of bed and said: 'Me stars are bad today - that's why I went back to bed - so if I draw the raffle I can't win it - and no harm done.'

So that night at the local, the club supporters gathered and

'*What did I tell you?*'

DAVID
LANGDON

Good Turn Jackson announced the raffle. He put the ticket butts in the hat and held it high in front of the Unluckiest Cricketer.

And Good Turn said aside: 'It's a matter of psychology. He'll win ten thousand quid, change his luck, and his complex will be cured.'

The Unluckiest Cricketer reached up and put his claw into the hat, stirred the ticket butts, all marked number seven – and drew one out.

The World's Unluckiest Cricketer looked at the ticket, held it up and yelled: 'What did I tell you? I'm a quarter of an inch off ten thousand quid. The winning ticket is number seven and a quarter and I hold ticket number seven.'

He had drawn the size tag out of the hat.

35

'Are you coming back on Monday?'

Fred Trueman

Like most fast bowlers, I fancied myself as a batsman, didn't I?

I remember as a young man playing for Yorkshire against Derbyshire.

Yorkshire batted all day and got a lot of runs, a couple of batsmen making centuries. It was on a Saturday. I remember it so well.

My Captain turned around and said to me: 'Freddie, I want you to go in as night watchman. I know we've got a lot of runs but if it happens to rain over the weekend on this uncovered wicket another thirty or forty runs on Monday morning would be a bonus.'

I was delighted. 'You want me to go in at number six?' I asked.

'Yes,' he replied. 'I don't want to lose another batsman. So, if a wicket falls, you go in.'

Well, the Yorkshire lads had fairly flayed the Derbyshire attack all round the ground on a beautiful day and a shirt-front wicket. There was a big crowd at Bradford and they were lapping up the fast scoring.

And sure enough, a wicket fell and I had to go in half an hour before stumps with orders to just stay there and not get runs. So in I went rather proudly. Even though I was night watchman, I felt I'd been promoted in the order, batting at number six.

Usually, I batted at number eleven: the only man who came after me was the groundsman with a brush or the roller.

I took guard and did as I was told, playing up and down the

line. I played some immaculate forward defensive shots but didn't get any runs for twenty minutes.

The crowd started to give me a right rollicking, didn't they.

A voice in the crowd shouted: 'Hey, Trueman! Are you coming back on Monday?'

After a pause, the voice answered itself: 'Well, if you are, I'm bloody not.'

And me thinking I was playing so well. Tell you what, if I could have taken a stump out I'd have crawled down the stump hole.

36

Famous Last Words: 'It's knocked the clock forward to twenty past four!'

Fred Trueman

One day, Alfonso Drake was bowling against the great Jack Hobbs, of Surrey.

Perhaps the greatest opening bat in living memory, Jack Hobbs could be a slow scorer when playing in a Test match, but he would often go for the hit in a County game.

Anyway, this particular day, Hobbs was really hitting out – and Alfonso Drake was taking a bit of stick, was Alfonso, and getting sick and tired of it!

Suddenly, at about twenty past twelve, Jack Hobbs, playing off the front foot, went bang and hit a ball from Alfonso high over the fence.

The ball soared towards the pavilion, so high it was hard to see it.

Someone yelled: 'Look! It's hit the clock! It's knocked the clock on to twenty past four!'

Alfonso muttered: 'A pity it didn't knock the bastard forward to half past six.'

37
The World's Best Cricket Umpire

Frank Hardy

The World's Best Cricket Umpire was a man named Andy Seal.

He had been a County cricketer before the First World War and, when the time came to retire, his choice of alternative employment was very limited. Outside of cricket, he knew little, so only three professions were open to him: an axeman cutting down willow trees for cricket bats, a cricket coach, or a cricket umpire.

Now, Andy was not strong enough in the body to be an axeman and not strong enough in the brain to become a coach - so he took up umpiring.

Andy Seal was a little bloke, walked with his feet at about ten past ten, had a very friendly nature, used terms of affection, and became one of the greatest name-droppers of all time.

He started his umpiring career in a very modest way in local leagues but was soon umpiring County matches. The reason for his swift promotion was that he made so many mistakes for each team - he liked to please everyone and balance things up - that the Captain of the fielding side always gave him full marks.

Also, he was grand company, was the old Andy, always good for a laugh, even when his humour was unintended.

Stories of Andy Seal's umpiring prowess were many and varied.

One day, early in his career, he refused three confident l.b.w. appeals in one over against Yorkshire (he'd refused a few for the other team and wanted to be fair).

Captain Len Hutton said to Andy: 'Listen, Andy, I'm

fielding at first slip and I'm quite certain that at least one of those appeals should have been upheld.'

And Andy Seal replied: 'You could be right, Lennie, old fellow, but I couldn't see a stump.'

On another memorable occasion, a well-known bowler was on the hat trick, Andy having given him a couple of overdue decisions.

Next ball, the bowler appealed loudly for leg before to get his hat trick off Andy.

Andy raised his hand and said to the batsman: 'As God is my judge, thou's out, too.'

Andy's sympathetic nature often shone through. One day, Freddie Trueman hit a batsman on the foot with a yorker and appealed for l.b.w.

And Andy said to the batsman: 'Aye, I'll bet that hurt thee, poor old fella, but thou are out, as well.'

An example of how Andy Seal liked to favour each team without bias, was the day he no-balled a fast bowler, who was going through the opposing side like a packet of salts, three times in one over – then called 'OVER' after the sixth ball.

The bowler complained: 'You've got to be joking: you no-balled me three times, so I've got three balls still to go.'

'Technically speaking, you have, old friend,' Andy replied, 'but you've done enough damage already and the game is too one-sided.'

Andy Seal had only one hobby outside of cricket and that was gambling. He loved a bet, did Andy.

So, one day, after he had refused appeal after appeal, a cunning wicket-keeper lifted the bails on a close stumping and said to Andy: 'I'll bet a quid that's not out.'

'Out!' Andy shouted without turning a hair, and added aside to the wicket-keeper: 'That's a quid you owe me.'

That great batsman, Joe Hardstaff, had a bad habit of walking on his wicket when he played the pull shot – and this led to an altercation with Andy.

Joe sometimes got away with his wicket-walking habit because umpires didn't notice his foot touch the wicket. One day, on the Melbourne Cricket Ground in Australia, Joe knocked a bail off when hooking a ball for four. Everyone, including the umpires, watched the ball fly to the boundary, but Joe saw that he had knocked the legside bail off. So he simply stooped down and put it back on again. Trouble was, a newspaper photographer snapped the incident – and there was Joe's photo in the paper next day, putting the bail back on with a sly grin on his face. He went on to make a century.

Joe Hardstaff had another trick to offset his habit of standing on the wicket when hooking: if he just disturbed a bail, he would run the first two fast, and when returning to his own end, run head-long, bat outstretched, and knock all three stumps flying in case a suspicious umpire should want to inspect the wicket.

Andy Seal had seen Joe get away with this trick and was always on the alert to catch him if he tried it again.

And, sure enough, Joe went for the hook and touched the leg stump with his heel and the bail was just disturbed out of its groove.

'Don't you touch these stumps.'

Joe had a quick look, ran the first run like a hare and came back for the second intending to send the stumps flying.

But Andy Seal ran over from square leg, stood in front of the stumps with his arms around them.

Andy yelled: 'Don't you touch these stumps, Joseph.'

And Joe Hardstaff couldn't very well, could he?

So Andy inspected the wicket and saw that one of the bails was on the ground.

'You're out, hit wicket, Joseph, old boy,' he said. 'And don't you pull that trick on me again.'

Andy Seal's reputation as an umpire spread and so did his propensity to drop names and use terms of affection. But some people were not impressed.

Like Alan Moss, the England fast bowler. One day, at Lords, Andy Seal no-balled Alan.

'Mossie, old chap,' Andy said. 'You're dragging your back foot over.'

'Bollocks!' Alan Moss replied expressively.

'What did you say to me, Mossie?'

When Alan Moss diplomatically failed to reply, Andy Seal approached his Captain.

'What did Mossie say to me?' Andy asked.

'Well,' replied the Captain. 'It sounded like bollocks.'

Andy was very upset. The next day, he was umpiring at Gloucester and Sam Cook, great spin bowler and mischief-maker, called Andy aside.

'Hey, Andy,' said Sam. 'What happened at Lords between you and Mossie?'

And Andy Seal said: 'That Mossie, do you know what he said to me, Samuel, old fellow? I no-balled him a couple of times, Sam, and he said, "Bollocks"!'

'What did you do, Andy?' Sam Cook asked, keeping a straight face.

'I'll tell you what I did, Sam, I reported him to the MCC. I put him in my report, Sam,' Andy Seal replied. 'By the way, Sam, how do you spell bollocks?'

'B-O-L-O-X,' Sam Cook spelt his reply out.

'That's what I put in my report, Sam.'

Anyway, Andy Seal eventually became a Test umpire and was officiating when the Australians came on tour in 1948. That was the last tour of England by Don Bradman.

And Andy Seal was in all his glory, umpiring the Test match at Lords, calling everyone by their nicknames, or full Christian names, inventing terms of endearment, name-dropping one to the other, without fear or favour – and, of course, giving all sorts of decisions.

Charlie Barnett made 99 before lunch and completed his century in the first over after lunch.

The first man to congratulate him was one of the umpires, to wit, Andy Seal. Andy walked right down the wicket and shook Charlie's hand warmly.

'Well played, Charles, my lad,' Andy said.

Don Bradman who, of course, was captaining Australia, said nothing.

Andy Seal then no-balled Ray Lindwall. Ray, with Freddie Trueman, had the smoothest action of any fast bowler in living memory – and was rarely no-balled.

So Ray Lindwall said: 'What did you no-ball me for?'

'Now, listen, Lindy, old son,' Andy Seal replied. 'You're dragging your back foot. If you're going to bowl in England you'll have to get back a bit and not drag over.'

In the second innings of that Lord's Test, Andy Seal met his Waterloo.

He was there, glad-handing, nick-naming and name-dropping in his best manner, when Don Bradman came in to bat.

'Hello, Braddles, wish you all the luck in the world, Donald, old son,' Andy Seal said.

Don Bradman said nothing.

Well, the game proceeded. Bradman, past his prime by then, was playing himself in, anxious to make a big score in what would be his last game at Lords.

Like all champions, Don Bradman didn't like to get out – especially on a doubtful decision. He was the greatest genius in cricketing history. Not only as a batsman and a Captain. But also as a selector. He wasn't content to help select the Australian team, he often had a lot of influence on selecting the English side, by dropping judicious and misleading opinions about players in the ear of an English selector. Many a man in Bradman's day, was selected when he shouldn't have been and not selected when he should have been·for the English team on the basis of Donald's oblique influence.

And Bradman liked to make sure he had the right umpires, too, a fact that Andy Seal should have borne in mind that day at Lords.

Well, Don Bradman had made about twelve when a ball struck him on the calf of his right leg. There was a half-hearted appeal.

Andy Seal, at the bowler's end, hesitated, then raised his hand.

'Sorry, Donald, old chap,' Andy Seal said. 'But you'll have to go.'

And Don Bradman said: 'Sorry, Andy, old chap, but you'll have to go, too.'

Recalling the incident over the years, Andy Seal used to say: 'I don't know what happened. Perhaps Braddles reported me to the M C C – but I never umpired another Test Match.'

But, Don Bradman notwithstanding, Andy Seal was the World's Best Cricket Umpire, wasn't he?

38
'The lads will be pleased'

Frank Hardy

Fred Trueman burst into Test cricket with the most sensational spell of fast bowling in history.

That was in June 1952, in the first Test against the Indian team, which was touring England.

In no time at all India were nought for four.

He recalls: 'Len Hutton let me bowl down the hill in the second innings and all Pankaj Roy could do with my second ball was scoop it into Denis Compton's hands. Alec Bedser had Gaekwad caught in the gully in his first over. Then I got amongst them, didn't I?'

Trueman took at least three or four wickets in each innings of the four Tests in the series – and gave notice that he would become the stormy petrel of world cricket.

The Cricket Establishment didn't know what to make of him – he doffed his cap to no one, and didn't call anybody Sir. One of the English selectors, presaging the attitude Fred was to suffer throughout his career, said after the first Test: 'I hope he gets nought for a hundred in the second Test. It will give him some idea of balance.'

Fred took four wickets in each innings.

Before the third Test, the old Frederick signalled the kind of self-assertion he was going to carry on with regardless. He said to Alec Bedser, his opening partner and a very skilful and experienced player: 'You keep 'em quiet; I'll bowl 'em out.'

One of his frequent victims was Indian batsman, Adhikari, who Fred reckoned turned white when he faced his bowling.

Twenty years later, they met again when Adhikari, by then a Colonel in the Indian Army came back to England as

Manager of an Indian touring side.

Fred greeted him: 'Hullo, Colonel, glad to see you've got your colour back.'

It took the Air Force to cut Fred down to size. He was in the midst of his National Service at the time and as he has already mentioned, he has fond memories of his stint in the Air Force and made many good friends.

After his sensational success in the third Test, he said: 'The lads will be pleased. I reckon they'll send a telegram.'

Instead, his commanding officer, who lacked nothing in the way of humour and irony, sent a telegram which read: 'Congratulations. You ended the Test early so report back to Air Force camp 8 a.m. Sunday.'

Report back

39

Famous Last Words: 'I've got bad news for thee'

Fred Trueman

The Yorkshire crowds love their cricket.

These two particular supporters never missed a match, always came early and took up a position near the sight screen. They took it in turns to bring their lunch, didn't they?

One day at Bramall Lane, Yorkshire had won the toss and decided to bat, when one of these characters said to his mate: 'Did you bring the lunch?'

Well, it turned out that his mate had left the lunch at home on the kitchen table – and refused to go back for it.

'I'm not leaving with Len 'utton coming in to bat.'

So the other fella decides to go and get the lunch.

When he came back, he said to his mate: 'I got bad news for thee. When I went round the side of your house to get the lunch, I saw your wife in bed with the butcher.'

'I've got worse news for thee,' his mate replied. ''utton's out.'

40

The Most Unique Record in the History of Cricket

Frank Hardy

Neil Hawke, former Australian all-rounder, had a successful career in Test cricket.

Like most cricketers, he would have liked to establish a record for something before he retired.

He played football as well as cricket for his state – but found the great Keith Miller had done that before him. He took more than 400 wickets and made more than 3000 runs in first-class cricket – but found others had done the same before him.

As far back as 1951, Neil thought he might have created a record. He had been summoned to the Adelaide Oval to meet Sir Donald Bradman and his son John Bradman. The week before Neil had made 111 not out in a District game and Sir Donald had been present – and decided to give Neil a batting lesson.

Well, after the coaching session, Don Bradman asked Neil Hawke to bowl to him in front of a white canvas screen while he illustrated the various shots a batsman should learn to play. Sir Donald was preparing a book on the art of batting, in which all the shots were to be illustrated with 'slow motion' pictures.

Neil still remembers the occasion well: 'I was to bowl the ball to a position where Sir Donald could play the particular shot he wanted to illustrate. But there were times when I didn't put the ball on the right spot but, such was Bradman's genius, that he would move and make it appear that it was in the correct position.

'While we were there, Sir Donald, for a joke, hit a ball hard towards the secretary of the South Australian Cricket Association and his wife – and it crashed against the wall of the changing-room inches from where they were sitting.

'He could put every ball just where he wanted to. And this was a man already over fifty years of age.'

Neil thought that might have been some sort of a record: being the man who bowled to Don Bradman when he was illustrating the cricket shots. But two other bowlers (names unknown) had done that before, because Sir Donald later gave Neil copies of two earlier illustrated books he had published with photos of the various shots.

But quite unexpectedly, Neil eventually established an all time Test match record – perhaps the most unique in the history of cricket.

And none other than old F. S. Trueman, his cheeky self, was involved.

The Australians were giving England some stick on the third day of a Test match during Neil's last tour of England. Captain Ted Dexter went into a worried huddle with Vice-Captain Colin Cowdrey to discuss bowling tactics.

Suddenly, the old Frederick strode over and he said: 'Give me the ball!'

Well, Dexter got a shock: Freddie had bowled a lot of overs in the innings and had taken none for plenty. Either because of the shock or because he could think of nothing better to do, Dexter gave Freddie Trueman the ball.

Fred paced out his run and with the fourth ball of the over clean bowled Ian Redpath with a beauty. To add injury to insult, with the next ball, he forced Graham McKenzie into error and he spooned a catch into the reliable hands of Colin Cowdrey.

And it was time for lunch. A dull match had been transformed and the old F.S. went into the pavilion on the hat trick.

Fred insists to me that he ate his usual hearty lunch with his team-mates that day. Other players state that he ate nothing but sat in the dressing-room puffing his pipe, nervous as a tom cat.

And Neil Hawke was the in-coming batsman.

Imagine the tension and excitement when Fred Trueman ran in to bowl his first ball after lunch.

It was not to be: Fred missed the hat trick. But word had

gone around the ground that he had begun the innings with 297 Test wickets – and he was on the brink of becoming the first bowler in history to take 300 wickets in Test matches.

And a few overs later, Fred Trueman bowled to Neil Hawke, who nicked the ball into the slips at just the right height and Colin Cowdrey did the honours again. Neil shook hands with Fred and began the long journey out.

There were joyous scenes, with the old Fred himself, hugging everyone in sight – amateur and professional alike.

Not much of a record for Neil Hawke: being the batsman who lost his wicket and so gave Fred Trueman his 300th in Tests!

That's not the record Neil claims. But that day, he established a record of another kind – and it's not likely to be broken for a long time.

As Colin Cowdrey pointed out: 'Neil became the only Australian batsman to shake the hand of an English bowler immediately after he had become his victim.'

41
'Always was your weakness'

Fred Trueman

After Bomber Wells transferred to Nottinghamshire, he was playing one day against Yorkshire.

And Brian Close was batting in great form. Closey had never made a double hundred but this looked like being his day.

He was 184 not out, wasn't he?

And he was seeing them well and batting with great confidence.

Bomber Wells was bowling off spinners at him and Brian Close was giving them some stick.

So Bomber bowled one outside the leg stump.

And Brian Close, a left hander, had a crack, and hit it high around to leg. It looked like a certain six, down the bottom end, near the West Stand, at Scarborough.

A lad named Mervyn Winfield set off around the boundary. He ran like a bat out of hell, about fifty yards. And just when the ball was about to go over the fence, he stuck his hand up and caught it. A brilliant one-handed catch – just as Brian Close was completing his third run.

And Closey was out for 186.

Bomber Wells clapped and yelled out: 'Well caught.'

And he turned to Brian and said: 'Always was your weakness, Closey.'

And Brian Close asked: 'What weakness?'

'Caught out in leg trap,' Bomber replied.

42

The Bad-Tempered Amateur Captain

Fred Trueman

This story couldn't be told - it happened in the 1930s - but for a battling professional batsman who had a large family and was so poor that he couldn't afford even a new bat, and an amateur Captain, who was so bad tempered that the County Club Committee, as well as the players, were frightened of him.

In fact, they are the central characters of the story.

On the eve of an important match, they each had a big problem.

The professional batsman's problem was simply a chronic touch of the shorts - and that was nothing new. He was just an average cricketer who earned barely enough during the summer to keep his wife and five children - and, during the winter, with the depression at its height, he was usually on social security. He badly needed a new bat - he was a pro and preferred to have his own cricket gear of good quality - but after a discussion with his wife he decided he simply couldn't afford it.

The amateur Captain's problem was that his opening batsmen, in the last five matches, hadn't scored ten runs between them in any innings. And he was livid about it. He was giving the players a hard time, wasn't he, having a right go at them.

On the day the match was to begin, the Captain gathered his players around him. They were nervous.

His eyes were as cold as steel and he said: 'I'll show you lot how it's done. I'm going to open the innings myself. And I've got a new bat for the occasion.'

Well, the old pros were chuckling secretly: they knew that

in the visiting side were two England opening bowlers who were real quick. They chuckled even more secretly when the visitors won the toss – and sent them in.

The bad-tempered Captain was only a middle-order batsman but the pros were delighted that he wanted to open: at least one of them didn't have to face the All England demons with the new ball.

Well, the amateur Captain put on his fancy cap, picked up his new bat and his silk batting gloves and said to one of the professional batsmen: 'You will open up with me.'

So out they strode to the wickets.

The battling professional batsman sat in the dressing-room looking at his old bat. It was battered and edged, had been bound up with tape and string dipped in tar, and all the spring had gone out of it.

And he was thinking: today might be my chance to get a new bat: if he says it again, I'll have a new bat for free.

So out he goes onto the balcony to watch the show.

The openers were approaching the wicket. The amateur Captain said to his partner: 'I will take the first ball.'

And the pro answered: 'Yes, sir.'

The Captain took his guard.

And the England fast bowler, a professional, looks at him and thinks: a fancy cap, eh, there's a wicket here – if I can bowl the first one straight; can't believe me luck.

With that dubious thought in mind, he added five yards on to his run up.

The bad-tempered Captain said: 'I'm ready.'

And the umpire said: 'Play.'

Well, the fast bowler set off on his long run and let the first ball go like a rocket.

It was pitched on a beautiful length, came in off the seam, through the gate the amateur Captain left between his bat and pads, cracked the middle stump and sent it hurtling twenty yards or more.

As the bad-tempered amateur Captain trudged his way back to the pavilion, white with anger, ripping off his silk gloves, he was a man to be avoided.

And the rest of the team were determined to avoid him.

The pro coming in one down didn't have to face him: he came out the professionals' gate and the Captain the amateurs' gate (the idiotic idea of separate gates still applied in those days).

All the other players, professionals to a man, vanished from the balcony and the dressing-room. They scattered in all directions: down the stairs, under the pavilion, into the toilet – anywhere just to be out of the way when he came in.

At such moments, the bad-tempered amateur Captain was capable of anything, even violence.

Any idiot who wants it...

So, as he approached the dressing-room door, the place was empty – except for the old pro who was so poor that he couldn't afford a new bat. And he was standing quite still against the wall near the door. He had often seen his beloved Captain in one of his tantrums and knew what was likely to happen.

Well, suddenly, the door is kicked in, and the pro with the large family stood behind it waiting.

The bad-tempered amateur Captain threw his lovely silk gloves in one corner, and he said: 'And I don't want any smart arse remarks from any of you lot.'

Then he realized there was no one in sight – and this made him worse.

He ripped off his pads and hurled them against a cupboard door.

Then he inspected his spanking new expensive bat, never used. And he threw it against the wall so hard it bounced back and finished up under the table.

And he yelled out to the apparently empty room: 'Any idiot who wants it, can have that bat!'

The words were no sooner out of his mouth when the old pro dived out from behind the door, crawled under the table and grabbed the bat.

He said: 'I'll have it, Captain, you won't find a bigger idiot than me.'

That bat lasted the professional batsman with the large family for three seasons; until he retired, in fact.

He never even got a benefit but he was fond of telling his friends in the dole queue that, at least, his Captain had given him a brand new bat.

43
The Worst Whinger Who Ever Went to the Wickets

Frank Hardy

I first met this bloke – the worst whinger who ever went to the wickets – during a country week match on the Melbourne Cricket Ground in the 1930s. He had a reputation of being a first-class batsman who had little luck.

'How would you be?' I asked him.

'How would I be? How would you expect me to be? I've had three innings in Country Week this year for three ducks. First day I got in the middle of a hat trick; second day I got me duck in a run-out decision which was so doubtful that the supporters of the opposing team booed the umpire; third day a bumper hit me in the chin, knocked me out cold and I fell on the stumps. I'm batting again today and there's a rumour that Harold Larwood is playing against us as a ring-in. Be just my luck for the rumour to be true and Larwood turn bloody body-line on me. And you ask me how would I be.'

Next I heard of him, his cricket career seemed to be going well: he had shifted to Melbourne and was playing district cricket – and knocking at the door of the Victoria team. But when I met him again he was working in a sheep shearing shed. I asked him the innocent question: 'How would you be?' Well, he dropped the sheep he was shearing, spat, and fixed me with a pair of bitter eyes and he said: 'How would I be? How would you expect me to be? Get a load of me, will yer? Dags on every inch of me hide; drinking me own sweat, swallowing dust with every breath I take; shearing sheep that should have been dogs' meat years ago; working for the lousiest boss in Australia; frightened to leave because me wife is waiting for me in Melbourne with a maintenance order. Was a certainty to be picked for Victoria this season

126

but they heard that I made a noise drinking me soup. And, talking of drinking, I haven't tasted a beer for weeks and the last glass I had was knocked over by some clumsy coot before I finished it. How would I be? How would you expect me to be?'

I met him next in 1940: we were in an army camp on the Caulfied Racecourse in Melbourne. 'How would you be?' I asked him. 'How would I be?' he replied. 'Well, I made it into the Victoria team at last, as you probably read in the papers. And in me first knock I had to strike that Eddie Gilbert, the Queensland Aboriginal, who bowls faster than Harold Larwood. Well, he takes the new ball, knocks the bat out of me hand and the middle stump out of the ground. The next week, Gilbert's declared to be a chucker and banned from first-class cricket; a week later, inter-state cricket is called off for the duration of the war; and I'm called up for the bloody army. And get a load of this outfit they've issued me with. Look at me flamin' hat: size nine and a half and I take seven and a half. Get an eyeful of these strides - you could fit a blasted brewery horse in the seat of them and still have room for me. And take a gander at these boots, will yer? There's enough leather in 'em to make a full set of harness. And it'll be just my luck to be sent overseas and bloody killed. How would I be? How would you expect me to be?'

Well, he did get sent overseas - and so did I. And the next time I met him was in Tobruk. He was sitting on a box, tin hat over one eye, cigarette butt dangling from his bottom lip, rifle leaning on one knee, cleaning his finger nails with his bayonet. I should have known better but I asked him: 'How would you be?' He swallowed his cigarette butt and stared at me with a malevolent eye. 'How would I be? How would you expect me to be? Shot at by every Fritz in Africa; eating sand with every meal; expecting to die in this God-forsaken place. And I'll tell you something else: they've organized an inter-unit cricket match for next Sunday. I'm playing for our mob as opening bat and it'd be just my luck for those idiot brass-hats to lay the matting wicket over a landmine and me be the first man to make a run over it. How would I be? How would you expect me to be?'

Well, he didn't run over a landmine but he was fielding in the outfield and, just his luck, a stray sniper's bullet picked him off. They abandoned the match and buried him with full military honours.

Then, one night in Tobruk, I had a nightmare: dreamed I died and went to heaven. It was as clear as a cinema screen. I saw him there inside the Pearly Gates and I asked him: 'Well, how would you be now?' He eyed me with an angelic expression and he says: 'How would I be? How would you expect me to be? This joint's not all it's cracked up to be. Get an eyeful of this nightgown, will yer? A man trips over it fifty times a day and takes ten minutes to lift it up to scratch his knee. And take a gander at me right wing: feathers falling out of it, I must be moulting. Cast your eyes over this halo: only me big ears keep the rotten thing on me skull. And just take a Captain Cook at this harp: five strings missing and there's band practice in five minutes. And I tried to organize a cricket match but I'm in a ward full of Yanks who've never even heard of cricket. "How would I be?" you ask. "How would you expect a man to bloody well be?"'